# HARDY AND THE EROTIC

**Series Standing Order**

If you would like to receive future titles in this series as
they are published, you can make use of our standing order
facility. To place a standing order please contact your
bookseller or, in case of difficulty, write to us at the address
below with your name and address and the name of the
series. Please state with which title you wish to begin your
standing order. (If you live outside the UK we may not
have the rights for your area, in which case we will forward
your order to the publisher concerned.)

Standing Order Service, Macmillan Distribution Ltd,
Houndmills, Basingstoke, Hampshire, RG21 2XS, England.

# Hardy and the Erotic

## T. R. Wright

*Lecturer in English*
*The University of Newcastle upon Tyne*

**MACMILLAN**

First published 1989

Published by
THE MACMILLAN PRESS LTD
Houndmills, Basingstoke, Hampshire RG21 2XS
and London
Companies and representatives
throughout the world

Typeset by Goodfellow & Egan Ltd, Cambridge
Printed in Hong Kong

British Library Cataloguing in Publication Data

Wright, T. R. (Terence R.), 1951–
Hardy and the erotic. – (Macmillan Hardy studies).
1. Fiction in English. Hardy, Thomas,
1840–1928 – Critical studies
I. Title
823'.8

ISBN 0–333–42528–6

To Gabriele

# Contents

# Contents

# Preface

In choosing a subject such as this, I am only too conscious of arousing and then disappointing false expectations. Hardy's understanding of the erotic, his transformation of desire into art, I should emphasise from the beginning, is an intensely serious business. It is also predominantly cerebral. The erotic, as I explain in the introduction, is a 'fiction', a cultural phenomenon, a product of human perception and distortion of the biological 'facts' of sex. Hardy both celebrates and deplores this distance between culture and nature, a difference which opens up vistas of voyeuristic delight and artistic play but also creates a tragic gulf between desire, which is subjective and insatiable, and fulfilment, which is always partial and limited by the contingencies of the external world. Disappointment, in other words, is an inevitable feature of the erotic.

I should also explain that this book focuses on the erotic world of Hardy's fiction. It does not explore the poetry, except where this relates directly to the prose, partly for practical reasons (there was no space) but also because the focus in Hardy's lyrics upon the departed moment, most evident in the poems of 1912–13, is fundamentally elegiac rather than erotic. My argument in what follows will be that Hardy's fiction explores both the delights and dangers of the erotic, displaying a growing awareness of the tension between his erotic perception of women as objects and his sympathy with their suffering as subjects. His last novel, *The Well-Beloved*, can be read as a final abandonment of the erotic delights of fiction, a closing of this particular phase of his writing. Much could be said about the erotic dimension of his poetry but that will have to wait for another book.

I should like to thank all those who have helped in the production of this book, including Frances Arnold for her encouragement, Gillian Beaumont of Stenton Associates for her careful copy-editing, and my wife, Gabriele, to whose patient understanding and tolerance this book is dedicated.

# 1
# Wessexuality: A Theoretical Introduction

It is difficult to avoid puns on Wessex and Hardy's main subject matter; his world, it might be argued, is at least half-comprised of libido. The term 'Wessexuality' is a recent neologism, coined in a review of a television adaptation of one of his more outrageous short stories (Black, 1973: 796), but Hardy's contemporaries made similar puns. A reviewer of *The Well-Beloved*, for example, complained that 'of all forms of sex-mania in fiction . . . the Wessex-mania of Mr Thomas Hardy' was 'the most unpleasant' (Millgate, 1982: 382). Victorian critics, who had been delighted by the dainty and enigmatic heroines of Hardy's early work, expressed outrage and disgust at the more explicit concern with sexual relations in his later novels (Cox, 1970: xxx–xxxvi). For most recent readers, however, much of the interest and pleasure in reading Hardy lies in his treatment of this central area of human experience. Hardy is 'almost unique in the English nineteenth-century novel', observes a recent critic, 'in that he creates women who are sexually exciting' (Stubbs, 1979: 65). In many ways, of course, his writing remains rooted in the Victorian period. But in some respects at least, as I argue later in this chapter, his treatment of sexuality both illustrates and anticipates not only 'the necessary conditions of loving' outlined by Freud, his contemporary, but more recent theories about literature and desire developed by such radical thinkers as Barthes, Foucault and Lacan.

It may at first seem inappropriate to submit the provincial master of Max Gate to the glare of exotic new Parisian theories, like Clym Yeobright choosing to return to Egdon Heath, but one purpose of this book is to test these hypotheses in sustained practical criticism. Hardy's work will be sifted, systematically but I hope not insensitively, for signs of displacement, the strategies and distortions of desire as it is transformed into literary discourse. The erotic I take to be a cultural not a natural product, what men and women make of

1

the biologically given, how they read each other as signs, investing each other with their own desire, and how they produce
artistic representations of their deepest wishes. Hardy, I contend,
is doubly representative in this respect, as a victim of the
vicissitudes of desire and as an artist capable of revealing its
operations. There is, as Freud said, 'a particular satisfaction in
studying the laws of the human mind as exemplified in outstanding individuals' (Wright, 1984: 39). Art occupies a central place in
Freud's system precisely because of its power to disclose, unconsciously and indirectly, the secrets of the human psyche.

Hardy's novels, as I hope to demonstrate, illustrate both the
delights and the dangers of eroticism; they portray the impossibility of undistorted relationships between men and women. Sometimes comically but more often with tragic intensity they serve
to undermine a number of liberal humanist myths about relationships, in particular the belief that sex, especially within marriage,
is the ultimate consummation of an interactive relationship
between coherent personalities. Images of coherence and com-
pleteness, according to Hardy, are normally the projections of
fantasy, which builds false images of self and others from the raw
material of inner needs. It is these images with which I am
concerned, especially the way men see women.

Hardy's women, it might be objected, have had more than their
fair share of critical attention. Studies of 'His Female Characters',
which epitomise what Philip Larkin, grumpily despairing of a
good Hardy critic, called the 'old-style approach' (Larkin, 1983:
169), go back as far as Havelock Ellis, who celebrated their
enigmatic fascination and 'piquancy' in a famous article of 1883
(Cox, 1970: 105–11). 'The type of womankind' presented in
Hardy's novels, Ellis argued in defence of *Jude the Obscure* thirteen
years later, had always been 'very feminine', full of reticence,
refinement, and the kind of sensibility which distinguished
'human sexual relationships' from 'those of the farmyard' (306–10).
Ellis, himself a pioneer in the study of human sexuality, was
perhaps the first to recognise the fundamentally artificial nature of
'femininity' in Hardy, its dependence upon cultural distortion of
biological 'facts', unlike Lawrence, whose celebration of the sexual
passions of Hardy's women owes more to his own notions of
female sensuality than to Hardy's. One critic went so far as to draw
an elaborate chart of the different 'types' of women represented in
Hardy's fiction: the vain and fickle, the ingénues, the hedonists

tending to neurosis, the highly sexed, the resourceful and enduring, and (finally) two pure women, Marty South and Tess (Guerard, 1963: 66). The point to stress here is that any such categorisation of Hardy's characters should not be taken as a description of what women are 'really' like, essentially and eternally. It is rather a (somewhat crude) representation of Hardy's insight into men's perception of women at a particular historical and cultural moment.

The presentation of women in Hardy's fiction, as Penny Boumelha has shown, has a deeply rooted historical and political dimension, needing to be seen as part of a wider debate about the nature of women and their role in society. Hardy's novels are full of explicit generalisations about the nature of women, their superficiality, irrationality and flirtatiousness, which have been taken together to reveal the depth and tenacity of his sexist assumptions (Rogers, 1975: 257). Rather more dangerous – because less easily detected as ideological – are the restrictions imposed by male images of women which combine their purity with their silence (Jacobus, 1979: 13), for these images help to create the world they purport to describe, moulding men's consciousness and limiting women's possibilities (Stubbs, 1979: ix). My concern, however, is not primarily political. I want rather to spell out as precisely as possible, with little overt evaluation, the erotic dimension of Hardy's work as illustrating basic processes of human perception and self-understanding under particular historical conditions.

This area is already quite well covered, most notably in Hillis Miller's *Thomas Hardy: Distance and Desire*, which focuses on the detached voyeuristic nature of Hardy's narrators and the way in which the characters' desires are in inverse relation to the accessibility of their object. But by treating Hardy's whole oeuvre as his basic structure, the 'whole' whose constituent elements he attempts to unravel, Miller loses not only the differences between different texts but also the tensions that divide the same text. Miller never allows himself to dwell in any detail on any single text, nor does he bring explicit psychological theories to bear upon a subject which cries out for such consideration more than most. His more recent study of *Fiction and Repetition* moves into this area, attempting to explain the function of recurrence, the compulsion to repeat, in two of Hardy's texts. There have been other studies of *The Return of the Repressed* in Hardy (Meisel, 1972), other attempts to bring psychology to bear upon the novels (Thurley, 1975; Sumner, 1981), even another investigation into their 'myths of sexuality' (Milberg-Kaye, 1983), which have contributed to my own. These and other debts will no doubt emerge in the course of the discussion, but I want first to develop a sense of the Victorian context of Hardy's work before considering some modern literary theories which have conditioned my own critical approach.

If Hardy was, as John Fowles claimed in *The French Lieutenant's Woman*, 'the first to break the Victorian middle-class seal over the supposed Pandora's box of sex' (Fowles, 1977a: 235), it was because he, with other contemporary novelists, began to explore a subject excluded from high art for a century, a subject often on Victorian minds but rarely on their lips. Fowles himself exposes the myth that 'the Victorians were not in fact highly sexed'; they were, he insists, 'far more preoccupied with it than we really are' but chose 'suppression, repression and silence' partly in order to increase the keenness of their pleasure, a secret delight which later generations have lost 'in destroying so much of the mystery, the difficulty, the aura of the forbidden' with which it was surrounded (232–4). His intuition is confirmed by Peter Gay's voluminous study of sexuality in the period of transition 'from Victoria to Freud', which 'invites the paradoxical speculation that the century of Victoria was at heart more profoundly erotic than ages more casual about their carnal desires and consummations' (Gay, 1986: 422).

The Victorians were intensely serious about sex, as about everything else. The word 'sexuality' is of nineteenth-century origin, developing from straightforward biological usage at the beginning of the century to the widespread exploration of the whole subject in medicine, psychology and literature at its end (Heath, 1982: 7–8). The Victorians too, whatever their queen may have believed, invented the words 'homosexuality' and 'lesbian-ism'. 'Pornography' also stems from the mid-Victorian period (1864 according to the *Oxford English Dictionary*). It is not therefore entirely true

that the Victorians, as is so often said, repress the topic of sexuality; it is, on the contrary, that they produce it, that with them the sexual becomes a problem which thus needs to be faced – thought about and investigated, explained and theorized, with medicine having the prime responsibility for this social task. (Heath, 1982: 16)

Voluminous tomes were devoted in the middle of the century to *The Functions and Disorders of the Reproductive Organs* (1857), spurious terrible-sounding diseases such as 'spermatorrhoea' were invented to describe simple nocturnal emissions, and female 'hysteria' was analysed in detail. But all this, of course, was 'scientific', betraying not a hint of erotic pleasure.

Even Victorian pornography was serious. Whereas libertine literature of the two previous centuries wrote joyfully about the delights of the body, 'Walter', the pseudonymous author of eleven volumes of anxious sexual autobiography, *My Secret Life*, privately published in the early 1890s, found everything more complicated:

> Walter runs through women, encounter after encounter, in order to know, to try to be sure, to grasp an elusive certainty and resolve the question of his identity as a man; the sexual is the problematic foundation of human being, the site and the trouble of existence as an individual. We have entered the age of sexuality. (Heath, 1982: 16)

The happy celebration of sex as 'good, clean fun' characteristic of John Cleland's *Memoirs of a Woman of Pleasure*, popularly known as *Fanny Hill*, even the tolerance of Henry Fielding for the natural passions of his heroes, have been replaced by a 'tormenting obsession' (Charney, 1981: 80).

*Fanny Hill*, of course, was driven underground in the nineteenth century by a form of unofficial censorship. No legislation occurred before the Obscene Publications Act of 1857, but by the beginning of the century it was clearly understood that selling obscene literature was a crime under common law (Loth, 1962: 105). Widespread bowdlerisation of literature, omitting (in Dr Bowdler's own words) all 'expressions which are of such a nature as to raise a blush on the cheek of modesty', and effective control by the big lending libraries and magazines in which novels were first serialised, meant that there was little need to enforce the law before the 1880s and 1890s when there was a whole spate of trials, including the prosecution of the publisher of an expurgated translation of Zola's *La Terre* and an unfortunate vendor of the first volume of Havelock Ellis's *Studies in the Psychology of Sex* (Stubbs,

1979: 18–25). This forced both writers and publishers to tread very carefully in their treatment of sexual questions.

Despite all this, the Victorian period was a golden age of pornography. While novelists who wanted to be widely read and respected (and remain at large) 'had to find less direct means of communicating the sexual component in the situations they described', resorting, like Dickens, to a variety of indirect literary strategies including metaphor and symbol (Marcus, 1969: 110–11), a huge pornographic industry was producing a torrent of tales about lustful Turks, amatory surgeons and other *Randiana*. As Stephen Marcus has shown, most of this pornographic fiction had little or no literary merit: page after page of organ-grinding, with 'unremitting repetition' and 'minute mechanical variation', absolutely no interest in characterisation (persons being treated as objects) or literary form (simply going on and on and ending nowhere, except in the case of *The Lustful Turk*, whose adventures end abruptly with castration). Language in such writing is 'at best . . . a bothersome necessity' whose function 'is to set going a series of non-verbal images' and auto-erotic fantasies (280–4).

Prudery and pornography, it is important to recognise, went together:

> The view of human sexuality as it was represented in the subculture of pornography and the view of sexuality held by the official culture were reversals, mirror images, negative analogues of one another. For every warning against masturbation issued by the official voice of culture, another work of pornography was published; for every cautionary statement against the harmful effects of sexual excess offered by medical men, pornography represented copulation *in excelsis*, endless orgies, infinite daisy chains of inexhaustibility . . . for every effort made by the official culture to minimize the importance of sexuality, pornography cried out – or whispered – that it was the only thing in the world of any importance at all. (286)

Such contradiction, Marcus argues, could not long continue, and he locates two main places of 'breakthrough': firstly Freud, investing sexuality with 'meaning' as the prime source of character development and of culture, and secondly the later-nineteenth-century novel, which also focused upon sexuality, depicting the anguish of individual characters struggling in such a contradictory society (287–8).

Hardy, of course, was by no means a lone voice in late-Victorian literature. The debate over realism which raged in France in the 1880s, with Zola as the champion of frank and accurate depiction of sexuality, found its focus in England in the work of such novelists as George Moore, in whose pages women 'seem to repossess their bodies in fiction for the first time in nearly a century' (Stubbs, 1979: 90). And if Moore portrayed women as victims of male desire, being forced by necessity to sell their major marketable asset, Gissing portrayed innocent, high-minded men struggling against sexual instincts which knowing and often nasty women were prepared to exploit. Less gifted novelists such as Sarah Grand and Grant Allen also brought the whole 'marriage-question' into the open, attempting to undermine the double standards of purity expected of men and women, while newly fashionable short stories by George Egerton, Ella D'Arcy and others depicted women with passionate longings for which neither men nor society made any allowance.

The husbands in Egerton's *Keynotes*, for example, are either drunken bullies or boring fools who fail totally to understand their frustrated, restless wives. 'By Jove, you're a rum'un!' mumbles one as his wife (who dreams of dancing naked before crowds of men) kisses him fiercely and bites his ear. She is reduced finally to helpless cynical laughter 'because the denseness of man, his chivalrous conservative devotion to the female idea he has created blinds him, perhaps happily, to the problems of her complex nature' (Egerton, 1894: 16–22). Another victim of male misunderstanding rails against the 'artificial morality' manufactured by men who create a perpetual struggle between 'instinctive truths and cultivated lies' (41). 'We repress and repress', she laments, 'and then some day we stumble on the man who just satisfies our sexual and emotional nature, and then there is a shipwreck of some sort' (57).

Hardy's own short stories, as we shall see, explore similar frustrations and shipwrecks suffered by passionate and impulsive women. He was linked with writers such as Egerton in a fierce backlash against 'The Fiction of Sexuality' which, according to James Noble, was full of 'foulness', 'indecency' and 'erotomania' (Noble, 1895: 490–8). Hugh Stutfield inveighed against 'Tommyrotics' (Stutfield, 1895: 833–45) while Margaret Oliphant suggested that he was part of a conspiracy which she called 'The Anti-Marriage League' (Oliphant, 1896: 135–49). Hardy himself felt that some of his contemporaries had gone too far. He noted somewhat mischievously in the margins of a copy of *Keynotes* that if 'real' women were as wild and passionate and removed from men's ideal conception as Egerton made out, it was scarcely surprising that marriage failed to work (Millgate, 1892: 356–7). He dismissed the work of William Platt, with its unpleasant mixture of masochism and necrophilia, as 'mere sexuality without any counterpoise' (Boumelha, 1892: 69–70). Wessexuality, the erotic dimension of his own fiction, is more than merely physical. It pervaded the whole of experience, which is what links it with the theory of sexuality propounded by Freud.

Sexuality for Freud was not simply a matter of physical 'facts', the sterilised 'scientific' language of Victorian medicine; it was a matter of desire, the libidinal drives which he claimed lay at the heart of character, of art and of all human activity. His discovery of 'the imagination of sexuality' forced him, for example, to admit that the stories of parental seduction he had at first believed to be true were fantasies with a meaning of their own, related very often to thwarted desires of the supposed 'victims'. While Hardy's admirer Havelock Ellis, produced his plodding *Studies in the Psychology of Sex* in the manner of an 'old-fashioned anthropologist of sexuality', collecting, compiling and cataloguing as many anecdotes as his friends could provide, anticipating modern sexologists in his naive belief 'that there is nothing that cannot be rationally understood', Freud offered an insight into 'human irrationality' at its deepest and most complex levels (Marcus, 1984: 225–6).

One of the most important insights of Freud's *Three Essays on Sexuality* (1905), and one which is particularly relevant to a study of Hardy, is his loosening of 'the connection between the sexual instinct and the sexual object'. In 'normal' sexuality, Freud explains, 'the object appears to form part and parcel of the instinct', but in 'The Sexual Aberrations', the subject of the first of these three essays, they are merely 'soldered together'. The instincts are capable of attachment to an amazing variety of objects, including children, animals and even, in fetishism, inanimate objects. Freud adds in a footnote that 'the most astonishing distinction between the erotic life of antiquity and our own' lies in the emphasis we place upon the object, finding 'excuses' for the instinct in the 'merits of the object' (Freud, 1977: 59–61).

Freud also stresses the importance of the visual element in the choice of a love-object, disapproving, in true Victorian fashion, of too much indulgence in foreplay: touching and looking are 'intermediate relations to the sexual object which should normally be traversed rapidly on the path towards the final sexual aim' (62). 'Visual impressions', however, he accepts, 'remain the most frequent pathway along which libidinal excitation is aroused'. They are also important in the sublimation of desire in art:

> The progressive concealment of the body which goes along with civilization keeps sexual curiosity awake. This curiosity seeks to complete the sexual object by revealing its hidden parts. It can, however, be diverted ('sublimated') in the direction of art, if its interest can be shifted away from the genitals on to the shape of the body as a whole (68–9).

Hardy's art is certainly full of celebrations of the female body though whether it sublimates or provokes such sexual curiosity remains to be seen.

Freud's second and third essays on sexuality, on 'Infantile Sexuality' and on 'The Transformations of Puberty', explore still further the complex process of 'finding an object' for the libido, the restless attempt to 'restore the happiness that has been lost', to achieve once more the sense of complete satisfaction experienced at the mother's breast (145). He also spells out in these essays the first version of what was to be called the Oedipus complex, requiring from men a transfer of desire from its initial object, the mother, to an alternative legitimate sexual object. Three later 'Contributions to the Psychology of Love' (1910–18) seem even more relevant to a study of Hardy. The first, 'A Special Type of Choice of Object Made by Men', begins by acknowledging the insights into sexuality afforded by literature:

> Up till now we have left it to the creative writer to depict for us the 'necessary conditions for loving' which govern people's choice of an object, and the way in which they bring the demands of their imagination into harmony with reality.

A great writer, Freud recognises, has special insight into the 'hidden impulses' of others and 'the courage to let his own unconscious speak'. He is necessarily restrained, however, by the need to bestow pleasure upon his readers, to 'remove disturbing associations' and to 'tone down the whole'. It requires science, therefore, to tell the whole truth (231).

Freud proceeds to spell out three highly unpalatable 'conditions for loving' which are exaggerated in a particular neurotic type of man but observable also 'in people of average health or even in those with outstanding qualities'. The first demands that there should be 'an injured third party', stipulating that a man 'shall never choose as his love-object a woman who is disengaged'; being desired by another is a central feature of desirability. The second condition is that chaste and irreproachable women never become love-objects, only those 'whose fidelity and reliability are open to some doubt'. Insecurity, in other words, increases desire. The compulsive nature of such desire is demonstrated by the third condition: that 'passionate attachments of this sort are repeated with the same peculiarities – each an exact replica of the others – again and again' to form a 'long series' (232–4). These conditions will be found to recur throughout Hardy's work, the third in particular sounding almost like a blueprint for *The Well-Beloved*.

These 'conditions of loving' are supposed to be 'universal', applying to human nature in all periods of history. But there is something particularly Victorian about the second of Freud's *Contributions to the Psychology of Love*, 'On the Universal Tendency to Debasement in the Sphere of Love', which analyses the failure of certain men to combine the two components of love, 'the *affectionate* and the *sensual* current'. 'Normal' development, Freud repeats, involves the transfer of desire from 'unsuitable objects' within the family to 'extraneous objects with which a real life may be carried on'. Where no such transition is made, however, 'The libido turns away from reality, is taken over by imaginative activity (the process of introversion), strengthens the images of the first sexual objects and becomes fixated to them.' The only release comes in 'phantasy-situations' in which the original sexual objects are displaced by imaginary substitutes more 'admissible to consciousness'. The real objects of desire, however, remain incestuous and the result then is 'total impotence' (247–51).

Less severe is what Freud calls 'psychical impotence', victims of which remain unable to fuse the affectionate and the sensual: 'Where they love they do not desire and where they desire they cannot love.' They can overcome impotence only by 'a psychical *debasement* of the sexual object' which destroys all resemblance to the maternal image. Women are accordingly split into two main types, the overvalued, idealised angel of the house and the debased prostitute. Freud recognises how severely his own generation is stamped with this pattern, institutionalised in its high ideal of marriage and constant resort to prostitution. He also sees that women, through 'their long holding back from sexuality and the lingering of their sensuality in phantasy', suffer from a similar association of sexuality with secrecy, 'the condition of forbiddenness' in their erotic life performing a similar function to that of debasement in men (251–6).

Freud the Victorian does not, of course, see sexual freedom as the answer to these problems. The easy satisfaction of desire, he explains, would only reduce 'the psychological value of erotic needs', which required obstacles 'in order to heighten libido'. It was the very asceticism of Christianity which had conferred such high value on love. There is 'something in the nature of the sexual instinct itself', he feels, that is 'unfavourable to the realisation of complete satisfaction'. Its final object is never 'the original object' (the mother) but always a surrogate, 'an endless series of substitute objects' which can never be completely satisfactory. It is impossible to 'educate' the sexual instincts, to adjust their claims to the demands of a civilised society; yet, he concludes, this very impossibility, and the consequent need to sublimate desire in art, can be seen positively as 'the source . . . of the noblest cultural achievements'. We may have lost happiness, but we have gained art (256–9).

There is no room here for a sustained critique of Freud, whose theory of sexuality was propounded only as a hypothesis which he was continually modifying, but he provided for the first time a powerful discourse, a set of terms in which the irrational motives of human behaviour could begin to be discussed. It is only to be expected, since both he and his patients were the products of Victorian conditions, that he should appear so very Victorian in his approach, earnestly grappling with the 'problem' of sexuality. Hardy, of course, was also a product of these conditions, which makes Freudian terminology particularly appropriate in tracing the distortions of desire, the restless search for a love-object, in Hardy's erotic world. Hardy did not read Freud; I am not claiming any direct influence. But he observed a similarly restricted society, albeit through the 'unscientific' intuitive eyes of a creative writer, probing the hidden impulses of others and letting his own unconscious speak.

Freud's ideas, of course, have proved immensely productive in the development of modern literary theory, as in the formation of modern consciousness in general. Any modern reader of Hardy brings Freudian insight consciously or unconsciously to bear upon the texts in ways that recent literary theories have attempted to articulate. Structuralism and psychoanalysis, for example, both point to the indirectness with which men and women structure their world in language, particularly in literature. The concept of the sign, at the centre of all semiotic study, highlights the distance between the conscious desiring subject and the external object by focusing on the arbitrary relationship between signifier and signified, sound and concept. The very entry into language involves the suppression of desire, since the subject is forced to adopt the symbolic code of his or her society, its given language. There is thus a constant distortion or displacement, analogous to that found by Freud in the analysis of dreams, between what the subject wants to say and what the language permits, between unconscious desire and what the censor allows.

All creative writing, according to Freud, is a kind of daydreaming, a fulfilling of wishes unsatisfied by life, a play of fantasy. The processes of selection and combination, which Roman Jakobson found to be central to all use of language, function at the literary level to produce metaphor and metonymy just as they operate in dreams to produce condensation and displacement. Words and images replace one another because of similarity or association through space and time (Jakobson, 1956: 76–82). Desire in language is therefore necessarily distanced from its object, refracted through distorting linguistic and psychological processes which show themselves most clearly in art.

One obvious manner in which repression or censorship feeds erotic literature is by enforcing indirectness, euphemism or circumlocution. Necessity thus becomes the mother of invention, producing the delights of what the Russian Formalists called 'defamiliarisation' or 'making strange', in which an object is 'presented as if it were seen for the first time', adding the attraction of novelty to something otherwise stale and familiar. 'Two white prodigies', for example, appear from beneath the blouse of one of Knut Hamsun's characters, an 'erotic riddle' not too difficult to solve but made sufficiently strange to provoke the pleasure of renewed recognition (Shklovsky, 1965: 18). 'Sterne's game of erotic defamiliarisation' in *Tristram Shandy* involves a similar set of hints and allusions, digressions and delays, which provoke the pleasure of suspense, putting off the disappointment of completion (49). The same process can be seen in the erotic literature of our own time which, even in the absence of censorship, continues to prefer 'the old literary traditions of evasiveness, circumlocution, euphemism' (Burgess, 1985: 399). Hardy, it will be found, is fertile in this kind of circumlocution, partly as a by-product of censorship and partly as a mode of literary foreplay.

A whole critical doctrine opposed to the fixation of meaning, the premature foreclosure of the text, celebrates the analogy between the reading and the sexual act. Roland Barthes contrasts that *jouissance*, or sexual climax, which in terms of reading has been called 'textasy' (Young, 1981: 32), involving a loss of the culturally conditioned ego in an active engagement in the production of meaning, with a boring rational contentment which comes from the passive consumption of a finished product. *Jouissance* comes only with the novel and surprising (Barthes, 1976: 40–1). Just as striptease is structured upon the delights of suspense and delay, although this is an oedipal pleasure which comforts itself with the knowledge that all will finally be revealed (10), so the enjoyment of a text involves unravelling the careful structure of the hermeneutic code, analysed in *S/Z*, in which mystery and enigma are carefully built up by a number of devices designed to delay the arrival at the solution (Barthes, 1975: 75). The point to stress here is that the enigma is a product of artifice. A whole superstructure of curiosity and interest is constructed upon a straightforward enough base (in the case of Balzac's *Sarrazine* the fact that the beautiful singer at the centre of the puzzle is a castrato). The questions, then, are more interesting than the answer. Similarly in fashion, another cultural system explored by Barthes, desire is a product of carefully designed artifice, stimulating the imagination to 'complete' the picture by supplying what is suggested but never totally revealed.

The analogy between the pleasure of reading and those of striptease is made explicit by the deconstructed Morris Zapp in David Lodge's novel *Small World*. Deploring the tendency of modern 'artists' to strip naked right at the outset of their act, which is 'all strip and no tease', he offers the principles of the 'classical tradition of striptease' as a 'valid metaphor for the activity of reading':

The dancer teases the audience, as the text teases its readers, with the promise of an ultimate revelation that is infinitely postponed. Veil after veil, garment after garment, is removed, but it is the *delay* in the stripping that makes it exciting, not the stripping itself; because no sooner has one secret been revealed than we lose interest in it and crave another. (Lodge, 1984: 26)

The ultimate revelation, if and when it comes, is bound to be a disappointment, an anti-climax.

Perhaps the most sustained analysis of the displacements and distortions of the erotic in fiction is René Girard's study of Proust, Stendhal and Flaubert, all of whom reveal the importance of rivalry and imitation in desire, the illusion of spontaneity or autonomy in the subject, 'the insignificance of the object' and the resultant 'disappointment which is called possession' (Girard, 1965: 39). Great writers, according to Girard, apprehend 'intuitively and concretely' the systems, the modes of perception, which critics and theoreticians attempt to articulate (3). 'We always think we move in a straight line towards the object of our desires and hates' but these novelists show us 'that the straight line is in reality a circle which inevitably turns back on ourselves' (74). Hardy's work, I hope to show, reveals as much as that of his French contemporaries about the way in which desire creates false images both of the self and of the pseudo-objects whose possession is inevitably hollow and unsatisfying.

Sexuality itself, according to another French theorist, Michel Foucault, is not a 'constant' of history but a matter of discourse, a language jointly constituted by the sciences that refer to sexual experience, the systems of power that attempt to regulate it and the cultural forms within which 'individuals are able, are obliged, to recognise themselves as subjects of this sexuality' (Foucault, 1987: 4). 'Discourse is not about objects: rather discourse constitutes them', providing the conditions of what can be said, the limits of what can be perceived, at any time (Sheridan, 1980: 128). The *History of Sexuality* as he sees it is not the conventional liberal humanist view of a gradual liberation from hypocrisy and restraint but the emergence of a discourse about sex which represents an extension of the power, originally of the Church but then of Medicine, to manage people's lives.

The confessional, Foucault argues, by encouraging sexual intro-spection, ironically helped to shape the narrative forms which made sexuality so much more exciting than the 'real thing'. The *scientia sexualis* then attempted to take over from the *ars erotica*, replacing mystery and secrecy by procedures for exposing what was thought to be the 'truth' about sex. But this too gave rise to new pleasures:

> The pleasure that comes from exercising a power that questions, observes, watches, spies, searches out, palpates, brings to light; and on the other hand, the pleasure that is aroused at having to evade, flee, mislead or travesty this power . . . all have played this game continually since the nineteenth century. (175)

No one more interestingly than Hardy, writing precisely at a time when what could be said and known about sex was undergoing radical transformation. The textual confusion of some of his novels occurs precisely as a result of the game he played with 'the Grundyist and subscriber' to the magazines in which many of them first appeared (Orel, 1967: 128). He campaigned strongly for the *scientia sexualis* in essays on 'Candour in English Fiction' and 'The Tree of Knowledge', a plea for open teaching of the facts of life (Hardy, 1894: 681). And yet his work relies heavily upon the secrecy and enigma essential for the *ars erotica*. It is not necessary to swallow Foucault whole, as it were, to see the relevance of his analysis of sexual discourse to Hardy's erotic fiction.

Another modern sceptic about the 'reality' of sexuality is Jacques Lacan, self-appointed defender of Freud's subversive tendencies against the wholesomeness of psychotherapy. The 'Real', for Lacan, is an inaccessible realm beyond the power of signification. All we can know is the 'Symbolic', the public domain of language, and the 'Imaginary', the illusions of unity, harmony and wholeness in which we like to believe. The stable ego, for Lacan, is part of the 'Imaginary', a product of the 'Mirror Phase' in which the prelinguistic child identifies itself first with the unified image of an adult and then with its own image seen in the mirror. The construction of personal identity is further advanced by the entry into speech, which gives the illusion of exercising control over the environment, calling people and objects into being and then dismissing them (as in Freud's famous 'Fort/Da' game) while actually creating a split between the subject in the grammatical statement and the subject who feels and speaks. The words, according to Lacan, never express the feelings fully or without distortion.

Psychotherapy, Lacan complains, can actually encourage false illusions of wholeness. In reconstructing his or her personal identity for the analyst the subject is in danger of 'objectification', creating a 'statue' of himself in a perpetual state of alienation. The art of the true analyst, therefore, is to study the discourse of the patient and 'to suspend the subject's certitudes until their last mirages have been consumed' (Lacan, 1968: 13). The same process of objectification takes place in the images we create of others. Desire, which is created by the absence of the beloved object (originally the mother), creates a series of substitute objects in an attempt to fill the void. It is not therefore 'a relation to a real object which is independent of the subject, but a relation to a fantasy' projected from within on to an external object (189).

What seems particularly appropriate to Hardy in Lacanian theory is the emphasis placed upon the visual, the construction of identity in the self and of others as objects of desire being based on visual images, seeing and being seen, the lure and the gaze. Sexual attraction, Lacan explains, occurs through the 'mediation of masks', visible images of the other that are filled with 'meaning' by desire (107). 'Desire', according to Lacan, 'is established here in the domain of seeing' and therefore vanishes as quickly as it arises, transferring itself to new objects in a process of constant displacement (85). Sexuality is therefore a matter of voyeurism and fantasy, doomed to perpetual disappointment:

> What the voyeur is looking for and finds is merely a shadow, a shadow behind the curtain. There he will phantasize any magic of presence, the most graceful of girls, for example, even if on the other side there is only a hairy athlete. (182)

Hardy too, I will argue, asks his readers to question what his voyeurs are 'really' seeing.

The indirectness of the relationship in Lacan between the libidinal drive and its object is captured in another startling image of a dynamo connected to a gas-tap from which 'a peacock's feather emerges, and tickles the belly of a pretty woman, who is just lying there looking beautiful' (169). There is no precisely analogous scene in Hardy but many of his narrators, as well as his characters, are voyeurs of this kind, creating images in order to satisfy their desire. Many of the objects of desire, the female characters, are observed in the process of looking at themselves in a mirror, which is traditionally seen as an index of their vanity but in this context (Hardy's novels as illuminated by Lacanian theory) suggests their search for identity as subjects, their attempt to escape from the objectification of desire.

For desire never ceases to fix its object, especially in fiction. Novelists from Goethe onwards have presented love as the framing of a particular image of the love-object:

> Stepping out of the carriage, Werther sees Charlotte for the first time (and falls in love with her), framed by the door of her house (cutting bread-and-butter for the children: a famous scene, often discussed): the first thing we love is a *scene*. For love at first sight requires the very sign of its suddenness (what makes me irresponsible, subject to fatality, swept away, ravished): and of all the arrangements of objects, it is the scene which seems to be seen best for the first time: a curtain parts: what had not yet ever been seen is discovered in its entirety, and then devoured by the eyes: what is immediate stands for what is fulfilled: I am initiated: the scene *consecrates* the object I am going to love. (Barthes, 1979: 192).

Such scenes abound in Hardy, whose heroines, as we shall see, are often portrayed through the eyes of their lovers, framed in a particular scene, glimpsed through a window, a hole in the roof or a clearing in a wood. In Barthes's words, 'Anything is likely to ravish me which can reach me through a ring, a rip, a rent' (192).

The question of *Desire in Language* is raised by another French critic who combines semiotics with psychology, Julia Kristeva. She too explores the way in which literature 'weaves into language . . . the complex relations of a subject caught between "nature" and "culture" . . . between *desire* and the *law* . . . between instinctual drives and social practice' (Kristeva, 1980: 97). Poetic language, according to Kristeva, struggles to rescue the instinctual drives repressed by a rational civilisation, but both language and the subject who uses it are necessarily fractured in the process. In Kristeva, as in other post-structuralist critics, the notion of a unified, coherent work of art is beside the point. The gaps and silences, contradictions and tensions caused by the struggle between desire and language are what matter. For 'one of the essential characteristics of literary language' is that it establishes 'a new relationship' between language and its object (Macherey, 1978: 43), abandoning false certainties for a recognition of the fluidity of our perceptual worlds. There is no such thing as 'pure' perception, especially in the area of sexuality.

These theories, complex though they are, seem to me to shed a new light on Hardy, whose work has often been criticised for clumsiness, confusion, incoherence and self-contradiction when it should rather be valued for highlighting the shifting, distorted nature of human desire. This book considers his fiction, predominantly his novels, but also his autobiography and his short stories, as a classic expression of the universal theme to which these theories all point: the distortions and displacements involved in the erotic fantasies men and women weave around each other. I begin with Hardy's *Life*, perhaps the most distorted piece of fiction he wrote, full of significant absences, omissions and indirect allusions. I then proceed to the early novels whose heroines, seen mainly through their lovers' rose-tinted spectacles, become victims of male fantasy, whether they die tragically or whether they are granted a 'happy ending'. Even in these novels, however, questions of sexual identity are sometimes raised, questions which are pursued further in the romances of his middle period, from *Far from the Madding Crowd* to *Two on a Tower*, which consider women more as subjects, exploring the self-consciousness of their heroines rather more fully than the early novels. They too are the objects of male gaze, but they are also subjects in their desire for men and in their search for an identity. The split in the subject to which these novels draw attention, I hope to show, is more than confused characterisation.

In Chapter 5 the focus switches to men seen by women and questions of masculinity. The virile Mayor of Casterbridge, for example, has been seen to be gradually 'unmanned', losing traditional male virtues while gaining in 'feminine' sensitivity. His passion for Farfrae is merely one element of a complex sexuality which he finds difficult to accept. The 'manly' woodlander, Winterborne, is full of similar restraint, in contrast with the philandering Fitzpiers, who gives free rein to his sexual impulses, gaining from the narrator a curious mixture of admiration and disapproval. Chapter 6 finds in Hardy's short stories, in particular *Life's Little Ironies* and *A Group of Noble Dames*, some of the more perverse aspects of human desire, its remoteness from all moral restraint and 'normal' behaviour. These bitter tales are not simply clumsy and melodramatic, as is often claimed. They deliberately subvert conventional liberal humanist modes of characterisation, displaying the grotesque distortions and perverse destructiveness of the sexual drives.

The climax of this study is provided by Hardy's three novels of the 1890s, which are given more extensive coverage than his other work since they focus so centrally on sexuality. *Tess of the d'Urbervilles* owes its eroticism partly to the indirections and circumlocutions required to pass censorship and partly to the narrator's obsession with Tess's visual beauty. She is literally silenced by being made an object for the eyes. Hardy's most tragic victim, she is reduced to the status of an object of Alec's lust and of Angel's impotent idealisation. Neither recognises her as a subject with desires of her own. The destructive power of sexuality is also the main subject of *Jude the Obscure*, which explores the unresolved debate of the 1890s about the nature and role of women. If Arabella stands for sex without the charm of the erotic, Sue is caught in a feminist dilemma, wanting to free herself from the fixation of male desire without denying her sexuality, attempting to celebrate the beauty of the body while struggling to escape from an inbred fear of sex. The constant revisions Hardy made to the text complicate still further this central split in her character. The two versions of *The Well-Beloved* give more playful expression to the whimsies and absurdities of desire, which flits unpredictably from one object to another. The later version, Hardy's last published novel, gives special emphasis to the link between such emotional instability and artistic susceptibility, the abandonment by the sculptor hero of his erotic daydreams bringing with it a loss of inspiration. Hardy's farewell to fiction, in other words, involves an implicit recognition of the indissoluble link between art and desire.

# 2
# Hardy on Himself: *The Life and the Loves*

It is easy to laugh at the lecher of Max Gate whose ghosted autobiography, carefully disguised as a biography by his second wife, distorts and omits so much of his secret philandering and fantasy life. Michael Millgate's recent edition of *The Life and Work of Thomas Hardy by Thomas Hardy*, painstakingly replacing what Florence tactfully discarded (some of his more wounded remarks about critics, lengthy lists of the nobility by whom he was entertained and lingering remarks on the physical charms of the women he met), can be said to reconstruct 'the image of himself that Hardy wished to project into the future' (*Life*: xi). But this image, as Millgate admits, is even less attractive than the original (xxvii), exposing him as a voyeur, a victim of the 'aberration' Freud labelled 'scopophilia', an extension of the 'pleasure in looking' beyond its *preparatory* function' to supplant the 'normal sexual aim' (Freud, 1977: 70).

Howard Jacobson's novel *Peeping Tom* develops this argument further through the critical eyes of his hero's second wife, Camilla, founder of the Alternative Centre for Thomas Hardy Studies, who portrays Hardy as one of those 'pathological romancers who see a shimmering new future in every woman they meet but are congenitally parsimonious with their seed', sheltering their timidity or impotence behind the 'tragic' demands of marriage in a hypocritical society (Jacobson, 1984: 143–4). 'What a humiliation it must have been for Emma Hardy', Camilla tells her impressionable pupils, 'to have lived with a man who yearned every day of their life together to channel his stream into another but lacked the force to do so' (179–80).

Hardy's two main biographers, Robert Gittings and Michael Millgate, also speculate on their subject's sexuality. Gittings presents a portrait of a mother-dominated adolescent shocked at

20

the 'unconcealed love-making' he must have witnessed at the dances at which he played the fiddle, dances such as the one in *Tess* at which Lotis is described as 'attempting to elude Priapus, and always failing'. Making much of a dream of Hardy's old age in which he saw himself on a ladder, trying to push a baby over the edge of a hay loft, watched by an amalgam of George Meredith and Augustus John, two of the best-known sexual symbols of their time, Gittings suggests that he may have 'developed sexually very late, if indeed he developed at all' and that this may account for his 'sexual curiosity, an attraction to the idea of love without the power fulfil it' (Gittings, 1978: 49–53).

Millgate too discusses this dream, seeing the baby as symbolising the burden of creative as well as procreative responsibility. He adds Hardy's descriptions of his dreams generally as 'like cubist paintings', usually ending 'with my falling down the turret stairs of an old church owing to steps being missing' (Millgate, 1982: 551). Quite what was missing even Millgate does not presume to say but he too describes Hardy as 'damaged, like Clym Yeobright, by so extreme an emotional dependence upon his mother' (22–3). Jemima Hardy, he claims, overprotected her sickly and isolated child, reducing him too often to the role of a spectator at the frequent family gatherings (42). There was, apparently, a family tradition that Hardy was sexually impotent, a rumour even that he carried a hereditary disease. Hardy himself, however, claimed to have been potent to the age of eighty-four (354). The story goes that when Florence Dugdale 'recited to him the last line of his poem "The Revisitation", "Love is lame at fifty years", he cried out that it wasn't true' (464).

All this speculation, of course, is fuelled by the obvious gaps in the *Life*, particularly where women are concerned. 'If one were to believe the Life,' as Gittings observes, 'Hardy had no contact with young women from the time he was sixteen to the age of twenty-nine, when he met his first wife' (Gittings, 1978: 17). This, of course, was far from the case, as the long list of 'Love attractions' in the index to Gittings's biography illustrates. The young Hardy appears to have mooned over a large number of 'village beauties'; the remoter the possibility of establishing any kind of relationship, the more he would dwell on their charms (48–9). The story continues with his affairs with the two Nicholls (jilting the older, Eliza, a lady's maid to whom he was more or less engaged, for the younger and prettier sister, Mary Jane). He showed an amorous

interest in his cousins, Rebecca, Emma, Martha and finally Tryphena Sparks, although it now appears unlikely that he was the
father of Tryphena's child. Then, after his courtship and marriage
to Emma, came the flirtations with a group of noble dames such as
Lady Portsmouth, whose attentiveness he always enjoyed (442–3),
a string of actresses including Mrs Mary Scott-Siddons, Helen
Matthews and Gertrude Bugler, the girl who played Tess, with
whom the octogenarian Hardy was hopelessly 'infatuated' (Gittings, 1980: 266), and a stream of aspiring literary women, among
whom were Rosamund Tomson, Agnes Robinson, Agnes Grove
and Florence Henniker, with whom he seems to have attempted
an elopement. Finally there was Florence Dugdale, who became
his second wife. Then, of course, the magic disappeared, for
Emma, his first wife, had recaptured the inaccessibility and
mystery essential for her idealisation.

Hardy remained a voyeur throughout his life, a connoisseur of
female beauty, whether in the '*poses plastiques*' in Leicester Square
or the paintings of Canova and Titian in the Pitti Palace (Gittings,
1978: 92, 281). There were also all the pretty girls spotted on the
train to and from Tooting in the early years of his marriage, not to
mention the young women 'in fluffy blouses' who distracted him
on the tops of buses (454). A notebook entry not included in the
*Life* records his admiration for a woman with classic features
glimpsed on the Weymouth to Lulworth steamboat, a woman, he
admits, 'I would have married offhand, with probably disastrous
results'. A later note suggested that she should be combined 'with
the girl from Keinton Mandeville' as 'Women Seen', the subject for
a possible poem (Millgate, 1982: 112–13). These women seen in
passing, whether on boats, trains or buses, gained as objects of
desire from the mystery accruing from the fact that he would never
know them. He did not normally make the mistake of marrying
them, but they fed his rich 'fantasy life' as well as providing him
with material for the novels. His description of Agatha Thorney-
croft, for example, 'whom he thought the most beautiful woman in
England', matches precisely a passage eulogising the qualities of
Tess's mouth (297–8).

Hardy's *Life*, in fact, displays much more self-awareness and
sexual awareness than his critics have allowed. It is a curious
document, full of reticence about himself and omissions, distortions or only indirect allusions to the major events of his life. I will
focus first on his presentation of himself and the great loves of his

life (his mother, Tryphena Sparks and his first wife) before proceeding to his analysis of desire. Not only in some of the passages carefully removed by Florence but in many that she let through Hardy displays a profound understanding not only of his own sexuality but that of his whole age. His discussion of prostitutes and music-hall 'dancers', of flirtation and 'sexual strategy' among fashionable women, of the role of mystery, enigma and unattainability in the provocation of desire, and of the struggle between nature and culture (or 'civilization') sheds a great deal of light on the 'necessary conditions of loving' described by Freud.

Hardy's treatment of himself is peculiarly impersonal, which is partly the result of the subterfuge of Florence's authorship and the consequent use of the third-person pronoun and partly of Hardy's extreme reticence and self-doubt. Given the scrupulous care he lavished on the preparation of the *Life*, it is customary to laugh off the claim in its 'Prefatory Note' that 'though often asked to record his recollections he would say that he "had not sufficient admiration for himself to do so"' (*Life*: 3). Not only would he pore over old notebooks before dictating to Florence, who would make notes for him to write up in full for her to type and him once more to revise, but he would also revise the final copy, adding and correcting details in a false calligraphic hand in an attempt to avoid detection. It was his major preoccupation for the last ten years of his life, stimulating much of his later poetry.

The *Life* itself includes a comment on the first years of the project: 'Hardy's mind seems to have been running on himself all this time to a degree quite unusual with him, who often said – and his actions showed it – that he took no interest in himself as a personage' (408). These statements, I believe, should be taken literally. Hardy did not 'admire' himself; he saw through his own pretensions as clearly as other people's and he did not take himself seriously as a 'personage'. One of the reasons the *Life* degenerates at frequent intervals into tedious lists of social engagements is that his public persona bored him. As he said of his earlier architectural career, he cared 'for life as an emotion rather than for life as a science of climbing' (54). The lists of London nobles by whom he was lionised should not therefore be read as a sign of social climbing and snobbery so much as 'a means of filling out the record of years whose really significant events – the onset of middle-age, the final desolation of his first marriage, the abortive affairs of the heart with other women – were too private and painful for public revelation' (xxv). These events, however, some of them at least, find their way into his poems and through them, indirectly and allusively, into the *Life*.

The women in Hardy's life, it has been argued, emerge 'unillumined, faceless and colourless' in the *Life*, a dullness only to be redressed by 'reading between the lines', in particular by picking up 'intertextual elaboration . . . on sexuality' through the many allusions to his poems, where his true 'life' is to be found (Morgan, 1987: 144). His mother, for example, occupies little space in the text. There is a brief description of her 'trim and upright figure' with its 'buoyant' walk which made 'strangers approaching her from behind' mistake her for a young woman 'even when she was nearly seventy'. Her 'Roman nose', he uncharitably remarks, 'would have better suited a taller build' (*Life*: 19). Florence adds some stories, gleaned from other members of the family, to illustrate the 'innocent glee' with which he and his mother 'would set off on various expeditions' (501), but she only really comes to life in 'A Church Romance', a poem Hardy includes in full since it 'expresses' her first view of her husband in the west gallery of Mellstock Church against the light of the setting sun (18). She appears fleetingly at various intervals in the *Life*, in particular at her death, but never with the intensity of feeling of which Hardy's later biographers write.

Hardy gives more space, in fact, to the unnamed 'Squire's wife' (Mrs Augusta Martin) on to whom his affections seem first to have been transferred. She 'had grown passionately fond of Tommy almost from his infancy', he recalls, taking him on to her lap and kissing him 'until he was quite a big child'. He adds, as if in afterthought, 'He quite reciprocated her fondness'. He certainly mourned their separation, when he was removed from the school she patronised, as from 'one to whom he had grown more attracted than he cared to own'. Although he was nine and she fifty, he confesses, 'his feeling for her was almost that of a lover' (23–4). The recognition that his feelings require qualification ('almost') before they can be admitted to consciousness ('more . . . than he cared to own') indicates Hardy's awareness of what Freud would have called 'infantile sexuality'. She later reappears as 'the lady of his dreams', necessarily disappointing the young man when he called on her in London (43) but still capable of stirring old passions when writing as 'an elderly lady' to congratulate him on the success of a novel:

by signing her letter 'Julia Augusta' she revived throbs of tender feeling in him, and brought back to his memory the thrilling 'frou-frou' of her four grey silk flounces when she had used to bend over him, and when they brushed against the font as she entered church on Sundays.

Hardy replied to the letter but never saw her again:

> Thus though their eyes never met again after his call on her in London, nor their lips from the time when she had held him in her arms, who can say that both occurrences might not have been in the order of things, if he had developed their reacquaintance earlier. (104–5).

The object of Hardy's affections is by now almost entirely imaginary, represented by a signature and the sound of her clothes, fetishistic products of culture rather than nature.

Hardy writes with more detached irony about the more 'normal' development of his emotions in later childhood. Aged fourteen, he records, he 'fell madly in love with a pretty girl who passed him on horseback . . . and for some unaccountable reason smiled at him.' He 'wandered about miserably' for several days, employing sympathetic friends to look out for her possible reappearance, but to no avail. It took more than a week, he confesses, to get over 'this desperate attachment' (29). He also 'lost his heart for a few days to a girl who had come from Windsor just after he had been reading Ainsworth's *Windsor Castle*, a clear example of the insidious influence of romantic literature. 'In this kind', he continues, was a similar boyish attachment to Lizbie Browne, whose bay-red hair, smile, voice and glance he was to celebrate in the poem he later addressed to her, regretting once more that he had let her 'slip' without touch of 'lip' (*CP*: 18–20). 'Yet another attachment' he adds to this list was a farmer's daughter named Louisa, who commanded his affection for 'a year or longer'. Florence on this occasion seems to have added the reference to the poem 'Louisa in the Lane', in which he longs to relive his meetings with her 'aspen form', no longer remaining silent as in their childhood encounters but addressing her with the tender affections he had felt (801). Florence also seems to have enjoyed adding the admission that in actuality 'bashfulness overcame him', limiting him to 'a murmured "Good evening"'. But 'the vision remained' (*Life*: 502), the imaginative product of Hardy's youthful desire.

The *Life*, of course, is completely silent about the Nicholls and Sparks sisters. Tryphena enters obliquely through a notebook record of writing the opening lines of the poem beginning 'Not a line of her writing have I' while travelling on a train in complete ignorance that 'the woman whom I was thinking of – a cousin – was dying at the time' (234). The main point of this poem, 'Thoughts of Phena', of course, is that the very absence of tangible records of his 'lost prize' – no letter, thread of hair or other relic – enables him the better to treasure the 'phantom' or 'picture' in his mind (*CP*: 54–5). Desire would be hampered by such real fetishistic 'objects'. The very obliqueness of the allusion in the *Life* can be seen as an intensely personal gesture, a 'way of speaking to the beloved, privately' and secretly (Morgan, 1987: 151), but it is hardly candid autobiography.

Hardy's account of his courtship of his first wife, Emma, also takes the form of a dialogue between different textual voices in which his own is somewhat subdued. He first transcribes her own romantic 'Recollections' of their encounter on the remote coasts of Cornwall, with 'the wild Atlantic ocean rolling in with its magnificent waves and spray'. Emma draws an equally romantic picture of herself riding recklessly in the rain, 'my hair floating in the wind'. 'The villagers stopped to gaze when I rushed down the hills,' she recalls with a certain pride. Opening the door to the eagerly awaited architect, she writes: 'I was immediately arrested by his familiar appearance, as if I had seen him in a dream' (*Life*: 73–4). For the lonely spinster, registering in the 1871 census as twenty-five when she was in fact thirty (Millgate, 1982: 123), Hardy was clearly the answer to her erotic dreams. Hardy's own record of their meeting, reconstructed from 'a few rough notes . . . entered in a memorandum book', is more prosaic, restricted to such details as her irregular features but perfect complexion, graceful movement and abundant, 'corn-coloured hair'. Her summer-blue dress, he noted, suited her better than the winter-brown she was wearing when they first met (*Life*: 76–81). He intersperses her recollections, however, with footnote references to some of the poems inspired by their encounter, not quoted in full but implicitly present through the allusions.

Emma's account of a walk to Boscastle Harbour, for example, in the course of which the two lovers lost a 'tiny picnic-tumbler' in a brook, is reported in the *Life* as 'versified' in 'Under the Waterfall' (*Life*: 74), a deeply erotic poem, also in the form of a dialogue, in which a lover is asked to explain the intensity of feeling evoked by plunging an arm into water and thinking of 'the purl of a little valley'. The 'chalice' from which they both 'sipped lovers' wine' becomes a symbol of the love ostensibly felt by the female persona but recounted by the male poet. The sexual symbolism of valley and chalice, it has been argued, is very much female while the male object of her affections 'lacks presence' in both these poems, becoming merely 'the disembodied object of female fantasies', a recognition on Hardy's part of 'his own indistinctness as Emma's lover' (Morgan, 1987: 55). Even in the account of his own romantic courtship, in other words, the *Life* investigates, albeit obliquely through intertextual dialogue, the fluidity of the relationship between desire and its object, the extent to which love is always an illusion.

Only indirectly, through allusions to poems such as 'When I set out for Lyonesse' (*Life*: 78), which celebrates the 'radiance' of Hardy's return from this visit 'with magic in my eyes' (*CP*: 293), does the *Life* capture the excitement of this courtship. Another poem he mentions, 'At the Word "Farewell"', suggests its frailty, for it is only at the moment of departure that her 'crimson' cheek betrays her feelings:

> Even then the scale might have been turned
> Against love by a feather. (406)

The *Life* says very little about the decline of their love, resorting once more to allusion (both to himself and to Wordsworth):

> The poem 'A January Night – 1879' in *Moments of Vision* relates to an incident of this new year (1879) which occurred here at Tooting, where they seemed to begin to feel that 'there had passed away a glory from the earth'. And it was in this house that their troubles began. (*Life*: 127–8)

The poem itself is hardly more revealing, dwelling on the wind and rain wheezing under the door. There is a hint of jealousy and some unconscious fear:

> The tip of each ivy-shoot
> Writhes on its neighbour's face;

There is some hid dread afoot
That we cannot trace. (*CP*: 438)

The main point seems to be that emphasised in the poem's final
line, 'We do not know'. Hardy offers no explanation for the
extinction of love and the death of desire; he merely records
it.

Florence, of course, Hardy's second wife, appears in the *Life*
mainly as its supposed author. There is only a brief mention of
their quiet wedding (*Life*: 392). She did, however, exert some
influence on the portrait of her husband as it was first published in 1928 and 1930, toning down or omitting altogether
some of the references to the physical charms of the many
fashionable women among whom he moved. Some of these
remarks seem relatively harmless, simply recording who looked
'remarkably pretty' (209), 'could honestly claim to be a beauty'
(229) or had a 'voluptuous mouth' (258). Others show more
insight into the distortions and necessary distance of voyeurist
desire, which is actually put off by too physical a presence. One
of the Florence-censored passages, for instance, discusses 'the
pretty woman of the party' at Lady Gaskell's: 'a fair, pink,
golden-haired creature, but not quite ethereal enough, suggesting a flesh-surface too palpably' and showing 'beautiful young
teeth' (230). Such erotic objects were clearly to be seen rather
than touched; on closer contact they might prove positively
dangerous.

Florence seems also to have omitted passages revealing Hardy's
interest in 'sexual strategy'. Among Lady Portsmouth's pretty
daughters, of whom Lady Catherine was 'the prettiest', with
'round luminous enquiring eyes', Lady Winifred is implicitly
rebuked for her propriety; she 'puts on the married woman
already', Hardy complains (209). Florence let through his lament
that 'women, even those who consider themselves experienced in
sexual strategy, do not know how to manage an *honest* man' (273)
but she cut his account of being treated as 'father-confessor on a
"wicked, wanton" flirtation' in which the same Lady Catherine
Milnes-Gaskell indulged (274). She allowed Lady Catherine to
define 'the difference between coquetting and flirting', however,
and to quote Zola on 'a woman whose presence was like a caress'.
She also let through Hardy's record of a conversation about
'passionate women . . . going on the streets' (275). One of her

neatest excisions, in fact, refers to prostitution, although Hardy's description of 'Piccadilly at night', with a girl holding a narcissus to his nose and an 'innocent family' waiting among the 'wily crew', loses some of its point without the two words which originally followed: 'of harlots' (247; see Bullen, 1987: 196). The contrast between the two halves of the Victorian psyche stands vividly exposed in this rich cameo scene.

Hardy clearly relished such cameos, enjoying the irony of overhearing 'a man coaxing money from a prostitute' outside the Temperance Hotel in which he was staying (215). He notes how appropriate it is that 'The Promenade of Prostitutes' should proceed along Regent Street, imagining the shade of the departed Prince Regent 'stalking up and down every night, smiling approvingly' (217). The most poignant scene with a prostitute, however, involves himself. Emerging from a respectable party held by a paranoid but 'very pretty' countess, he is forced by a cab strike to take a bus back to South Kensington, travelling on the open upper deck:

> No sooner was I up there than the rain began. A girl who had scrambled up after me asked for the shelter of my umbrella, and I gave it, – when she startled me by holding on tight to my arm and bestowing on me many kisses for the trivial kindness. She told me she had been to 'The Pav', and was tired, and was going home. She had not been drinking. I descended at the South Kensington Station and watched the 'bus bearing her away. An affectionate nature wasted on the streets! (281)

All Hardy's insecurity (he has to reassure himself that she kisses him out of gratitude, not drink), his relish of a 'natural' act and his nostalgic memory of the fleeting unrepeatable moment emerge in this short passage.

Hardy, of course, was no stranger to places such as the Cider Cellars in Leicester Square, where mock prostitute trials were held (43). He also records his 'humour for going the round of the Music-halls', pronouncing upon the beauties 'whose lustrous eyes and pearly countenances show that they owe their attractions to art', for they are 'seldom well-formed physically' (237). He complains that the dancing-girls at the 'Empire' are 'skeletons', in need of a month's fattening 'to round out their beauty' (265). At the Moulin Rouge in Paris he observes a 'strangely bizarre effect':

that the cemetery of Montmartre is visible through the back windows over the heads of 'the young women dancing the *cancan*, and grimacing at the men' (240), the shadow of death casting a characteristic gloom over the artifice of desire. He portrays himself in all these scenes as sardonically self-conscious, aware of the absurdity of such erotic performances even while he patronises them.

Hardy also shows himself to be aware of the whole syndrome of psychical impotence from which he and his generation suffer. He describes in Swinburnean hyperbole a young lady encountered at Walter Pater's: 'an Amazon; more, an Atalanta; most a Faustina. Smokes: Handsome girl: cruel small mouth: she's of the class of interesting women one would be afraid to marry' (221). Proximity and availability, he recognises, would not only dampen his ardour but exhaust his capability. He lingers over the beauty of a girl glimpsed on a bus, aware that she is an image on to which his desire projects itself:

> That girl in the omnibus had one of those faces of marvellous beauty which are seen casually in the streets but never among one's friends. It was perfect in its softened classicality: a Greek face translated into English. Moreover she was fair, and her hair pale chestnut. Where do these women come from? Who marries them? Who knows them? (288)

The answer to these questions, of course, is nobody, since they have no 'real' existence but are figments of his imagination, images to be appropriated and filled with unsatisfied desire. But the questions do not require an answer; their function is to create the mystery and enigma on which eroticism thrives.

Perhaps most revealing of all Hardy's generalisations about love in the *Life* is one recorded about the time of writing *Tess* in which he recognises that true love requires the abandonment of the false visions and projections of desire:

> It is the incompleteness that is loved, when love is sterling and true. This is what differentiates the real one from the imaginary, the practical from the impossible, the Love who returns the kiss from the Vision that melts away. A man sees the Diana or Venus in his beloved, but what he loves is the difference. (251)

Unlike Lacan, whose distinction between the real and the imaginary recognises the distortions created by desire, Hardy here, as in his most famous novel, holds out the possibility of genuine love and real relationship if only as a goal seldom achieved.

Another major theme common to *Tess* and the *Life* (and to most of Hardy's writing) is that of the clash between nature and civilisation. Sometimes this comes down to the difference between Wessex and London, as in his description of the 'quadrille class' at Weymouth, 'where a good deal of flirtation went on, the so-called "class" being, in fact, a gathering for dancers and love-making by adepts of both sexes'. Hardy, it is recorded, 'found the young ladies of Weymouth heavier on the arm than their London sisters', presumably a matter as much of their relative lack of sophistication and detachment as their physical weight (66). Similarly, at Sturminster Norton on Coronation Day in 1877, he notices the naive and open sexuality of the local girls, their innocent enjoyment of the dance:

> The pretty girls, just before a dance, stand in inviting postures on the grass. As the couples in each figure pass near where their immediate friends loiter, each girl-partner gives a laughing glance at such friends, and whirls on. (118)

He notices too how four itinerant musicians seen in Dorchester some years later, one of whom had 'a fixed, old, hard face' and another 'rather bold dark eyes, and a coquettish mouth', are transfigured by the light of a silversmith's shop: '*Now* they were what nature had made them, before the smear of "civilization" had sullied their existences.' Rural life, he continues, 'may reveal coarseness' but not 'that libidinousness that makes the scum of cities so noxious' (171).

This moralistic tone surfaces quite often in Hardy's description of London ladies, whose veneer of respectability often fails to mask a rampant sexuality. A description of a service at St Mary Abbots, Kensington, brings out this hypocrisy through a wealth of visual images:

> The red plumes and ribbon in two stylish girls' hats in the foreground match the red robes of the persons round Christ on the Cross in the east window. The pale crucified figure rises up from a parterre of London bonnets and artificial hair-coils.

Hardy's indignation rises as he begins to speculate on the real
subject of their thoughts, the powerful subcurrents beneath the
pious exteriors:

> When the congregation rises there is a rustling of silks like that
> of the Devils' wings in Paradise Lost. Every woman then, even if
> she had forgotten it before, has a single thought to the folds of
> her clothes. They pray in the liturgy as if under enchantment.
> Their real life is spinning on beneath this apparent one of calm,
> like the District Railway-trains underground just by – throbbing
> rushing, hot, concerned with next week, last week. Could these
> true scenes in which this congregation is living be brought into
> church bodily with the personages, there would be a churchful
> of jostling phantasmagorias crowded like a heap of soap bub-
> bles, infinitely intersecting, but each seeing only his own. (219)

The private world of these fashionable ladies is deeply erotic, the
concern with clothes being the mere surface of their subconscious
preoccupation with sex, powerfully captured in the symbolic
throbbing underground trains.

Another service, this time at St George's, Hanover Square, sets
Hardy brooding once more on these rapacious women of 'civilized' society:

> Coming out of church he went into the Criterion for supper,
> where, first going to the second floor, he stumbled into a room
> whence proceeded 'low laughter and murmurs, the light of
> lamps with pink shades; where the men were all in evening
> clothes, ringed and studded, and the women much uncovered in
> the neck and heavily jewelled, their glazed and lamp-blacked
> eyes wandering'. He descended and had his supper in the
> grill-room. (236)

The artificial light, the elaborate state of undress and, most
significantly, the glazed, dark and wandering eyes, quite literally
spoil his appetite. His recognitions of the beauty of such society
ladies are interspersed with exclamations at their distance from
nature: 'But these women! If put into rough wrappers in a
turnip-field, where would their beauty be?' (235). On seeing an
elaborate landau and pair bearing 'the *petite* figure of the owner's

young wife in violet velvet and silver trimming', he speculates on the excessive cultural wrapping of the original natural object, 'who, if held up by the hair and slipped out of her clothes, carriage, etc. etc. . . . would not be much larger than a skinned rabbit, and of less use' (249).

Hardy, of course, is trying to have it both ways. No one admires or enjoys more than he the erotic sophistication which culture bestows upon nature. Yet he knows and records the fact that it is artificial, a product of ingenuity on the one side and imagination on the other. His novels, as I hope to show, create and explore an erotic world riddled with similar contradictions, in which the distance between the phantoms projected by desire and the real objects on which they are based becomes increasingly more obvious. Hardy hankers constantly to return to 'nature' in works which are themselves a prime example of distorted yet beautiful culture.

# 3

# Obscure Objects of Desire: The Early Novels

The heroines of Hardy's early novels are presented primarily as objects of erotic interest not only for the narrators and for the male characters through whom they are observed but also for the implied reader/voyeur. They are described in visual, even pictorial terms as seen through the tinted spectacles of their lovers' fantasies. As characters they tend to be shallow, enigmatic and inconsistent. What they think or feel seems not to matter; the focus of attention is on the feelings they arouse in a variety of men, the misapprehensions they provoke, whether deliberately or not, and the virtual impossibility of establishing anything approaching reciprocity of relationship. Too many illusions, too many false pictures, have been created in the eyes of the male voyeurs for there to be much awareness of these women as subjects.

## THE POOR MAN AND THE LADY

The basic structure of Hardy's novels, it has been pointed out, is that of *The Poor Man and the Lady*. The plot of each of his novels can be described in terms of whether the poor man wins the lady, misses her, or turns instead to a 'non-lady', someone of his own class (Hyde, 1969: 14–18). *The Poor Man and the Lady* is, of course, the title of his first novel, finished in 1868 but published only in the form of a short story, 'An Indiscretion in the Life of an Heiress', ten years later. Among the reasons for Macmillan's rejection of the novel, apart from its political satire, were the 'disgusting' sexual details of the 'violation of a young lady at an evening party, and the subsequent birth of a child'. The aspiring author was advised to set such unpleasant scenes further away from the drawing-rooms of London, in 'foreign countries', if they had to be included at all. The story, according to Morley, was altogether too much of 'a clever lad's dream' and had to be severely censored (Morgan, 1943: 88–94).

There is certainly a dreamlike quality about 'An Indiscretion in the Life of an Heiress', apparent not only in its melodramatic and seemingly unconnected events but also in the treatment of its heroine, whose visual attractions become the image or 'film' of her lover's erotic fantasy. Geraldine Allenville is presented as an object of beauty from the very first scene, in which the schoolmaster, Egbert Mayne, stares at her with 'fixity of gaze' during the evening service in their parish church. In the gathering darkness her face begins to resemble the carved marble skull close to her head, an index not only of the tragic end in store for her but of the static, statuesque, objectified status she assumes in the eyes of her admirer. Ever since rescuing her from a threshing-machine the previous week, we are told, he had been filled with desire not only to 'possess' her but to 'exhibit' her, which is again more appropriate for a work of art than a human being (*ILH*: 29–33).

The schoolmaster's fixation is increased when she visits his classroom:

> To his eyes her beauty was indescribable. . . . The clear, deep eyes, full of all tender expressions; the fresh, subtly-curved cheek, changing its tones of red with the fluctuation of each thought; the ripe tint of her delicate mouth, and the indefinable line where lip met lip; the noble bend of her neck, the wavy lengths of her dark brown hair, the soft motions of her bosom when she breathed, the light fall of her little feet, the elegances of her attire, all struck him as something he had dreamed of and was not actually seeing. (35–36).

The last line is crucial. For what he 'sees' is not so much her face as the reflection of his desire, which alights upon the conventional requirements of dainty feet and swelling bosom, delicate mouth and wavy hair. The same process takes place with her words of farewell: 'though he knew the plain import of the words, he could not help toying with them, looking at them from all points, and investing them with extraordinary meanings' (39). She is a text to be read with *jouissance*, abandoning all notion of intended or inherent meaning. She has become part of an erotic dream.

The narrative clearly recognises the unreality of Mayne's emotions, which 'burnt' in ever 'wilder worship'. The difference of rank between them provides the 'great condition of idealization in love', a physical and social separation which keeps 'the petty human elements that enter into life . . . entirely out of sight' (46). They meet seldom and briefly, a consciousness of the attraction she holds for him causing Geraldine's heart to 'palpitate . . . whenever he came near' (47). She is, like Hardy's most famous heroine, 'reckless though pure' and smothered in images drawn from nature: 'a passionate liking for his society', for example, creeps over her 'like ripeness over fruit' (48). But as with Tess, the focus of attention is not on what she says but on the shape of the words 'upon her lips' (50).

When Mayne returns to the village after a five-year absence in London it is the surface texture of her image which once again fascinates him, as he comes close enough to her during a performance of the *Messiah* to hear 'the rustle of her garments' and the 'murmur of her words' (86). That the lady he loves is a figment of his imagination becomes all too obvious on the morning of her wedding to someone of her own class. Egbert, lying in bed, 'conjured up the image of Geraldine', falling into a dream in which her 'form appeared flitting about . . . getting thinner and thinner till she was a mere film tossed about upon a seething mass' (108). It is almost an anticipation of pornographic cinema. The film, in this case, is provided by the visual memory of her fair form, which is the screen on which the 'seething mass' of his desire fixes its gaze.

The poor man finally possesses his lady when they elope together, but only briefly. He is left a powerless spectator, gazing from the summerhouse and attempting to interpret the meaning of her outline in the door and windows of the house as she pleads in vain for reconciliation with her father before collapsing and dying from a ruptured blood vessel. The narrator imposes a tragic meaning on the text, portraying her feeble struggles for life as 'a silent wrestling with all the powers of the universe' (125). More significant, however, than this arbitrary ending is the lack of reciprocity throughout the relationship. The lady has never been more than an object of the poor man's lingering gaze. This is not to say, with traditional liberal humanist critics, that it is an example of 'poor characterisation'. It is rather a dramatisation, an objectification, of the processes of male desire.

## DESPERATE REMEDIES

Hardy's first published novel, *Desperate Remedies*, was also rejected by Macmillan on account of its 'disgusting' and 'extravagant' scenes (Morgan, 1943: 43–4). It too dwells on the visual, how things appear to the eyes of a beholder, as in its opening chapter, in which Cytherea Graye watches helplessly through a window as her father falls to his death from some scaffolding. The reader is constantly encouraged 'to share the character's or narrator's role as viewer or *voyeur*', glimpsing the action as so often in Hardy 'through peepholes or up chimneys or down wells or in mirrors', in static scenes or 'snapshots' in which the action is frozen as if by a painting or photograph (Page, 1977: 93). Cytherea in particular is repeatedly described in terms of the pictorial, sitting by an open window leaning upon a sill 'like another Blessed Damozel' (*DR*: 98) or looking over her shoulder 'with a faint accent of reproach' as in Greuze's *Head of a Girl*. The male narrator cannot conceal his own excitement over this particular posture, adopting a teasing flirtatious pose of his own:

> It is not for a man to tell fishers of men how to set out their fascinations so as to bring about the highest possible average of takes within the year: but the action that tugs hardest of all at an emotional beholder is this sweet method of turning which steals the bosom away and leaves the eyes behind. (89)

The metaphors of angling and selling, together with the narrator's false modesty, should not be allowed to obscure the force of the ending here, which recognises the importance both of the loving look and of the concealed object of desire.

Cytherea Graye is involved in three very different love relationships: first with a young architect, Edward Springrove; secondly with her mistress, Miss Aldclyffe, and thirdly with the villain of the piece, Aeneas Manston. Her identity, her image of herself and the image her lovers have of her, differs in all three. In Springrove's eyes she attains an integrity, a unity of image which is clearly an illusion. 'How blissful it is at first,' comments the world-weary narrator, as the young man offers impulsively to take her out in a boat,

> before reflection has set in . . . when on the man's part the mistress appears to the mind's eye in picturesque, hazy, and

fresh morning lights . . . when, as yet, she is known only as the
wearer of one dress, which shares her own personality; as the
stander in one special position, the giver of one bright particular
glance, and the speaker of one tender sentence. (74–5)

Such harmony and unity of image, so static as to approach the
condition of a photograph or painting and nearly as silent, is
bound to be destroyed.

To begin with, however, the young lovers are able to indulge
their illusions of harmony. Springrove meets Cytherea's blushing
glance with 'an ardent fixed gaze' while she enjoys the excitement
of his suggestive physical proximity, as he lunges rhythmically
forwards and backwards while rowing her further and further
from the firm ground of moral respectability. Each time he leans
forward 'her vivid imagination began to thrill her with a fancy that
he was going to clasp his arms around her' (75). Outwardly, of
course, she behaves with the modesty and decorum expected of a
lady, growing quickly embarrassed and pulling the tiller-rope to
bring them back to shore, but she cannot conceal her excitement as
his 'warm breath fanned and crept round her face like a caress'
(76).

The narrative extracts every ounce of erotic suspense and delay
as Springrove abandons his oars and seats himself next to
Cytherea. Their every movement is meticulously observed, leading slowly to its eventual climax:

> She breathed more quickly and warmly: he took her right hand
> in his own right: it was not withdrawn. He put his left hand
> behind her neck till it came round upon her left cheek: it was not
> thrust way. Lightly pressing her, he brought her face and mouth
> towards his own; when, at this the very brink, some unaccount-
> able thought or spell within him suddenly made him halt – even
> now, and as it seemed as much to himself as to her, he timidly
> whispered 'May I?' (80–1)

Her reply overcomes the limits of language, 'a No from so near the
affirmative frontier as to be affected with the Yes accent', drawn
out, we are expected to believe, for 'nearly a quarter of a minute'
and sounding 'like the spring coo of a pigeon on unusually
friendly terms with its mate'. Springrove needs no further invi-
tation and the kiss finally comes. It is 'the supremely happy

moment of their experience', endowing their 'lineaments' with the 'purple light' of love (81). There is a literary allusion here, not only to Virgil but to the queen in Gray's 'Progress of Poetry', over whose 'warm cheek' and 'rising bosom move/The bloom of young Desire, and purple light of Love' (15). But the scene is primarily visual, capturing the particular moment when the lovers are entwined and literally transfigured in the evening sunlight, as in a painting or photograph.

The rest of the novel can be seen as an attempt to recapture the unity and integrity of this moment against all the forces which conspire to keep the lovers apart, to fracture that harmony. Cytherea tries to capture her feelings on paper but is persuaded by Miss Aldclyffe to tear her love-letter into little pieces, 'mutilated forms without meaning' which 'his eye would never read' (125). When she does write, to advise him to marry his earlier love, it is only by reading between the lines that he can see that it 'unconsciously . . . betrayed a lingering tenderness of love at every unguarded turn' (170). Miss Aldclyffe, however, persuades him that what he reads as 'suppressed love' is only 'kindness of tone' (228) and he renounces her. Their images are reunited on the morning immediately after her marriage to Manston, but distorted and inverted in their reflection in a stream by which they meet. It is only at the very end of the novel, after all the obstacles to their union have been overcome, by repeating their evening row in a boat and every detail of their first kiss, that they piece together the fragments of their fractured love, reading each other's full meaning and reconstructing the visual image of harmony and wholeness.

One of the complications which disturb this harmony in the course of the novel is Cytherea's relationship with Miss Aldclyffe. Critics find it hard to believe that Hardy 'realised that he was portraying an apparently Lesbian attachment' (Taylor, 1982: 15), suggesting that he was merely recounting an actual experience of his cousin's (Gittings, 1978: 206) and unconsciously 'blundering in the pre-Freudian darkness' (Millgate, 1971: 173). Much is made of the emphasis on Miss Aldclyffe's motherliness, as if this precluded erotic attraction. Having been Cytherea's 'mother's rival' for her father's hand (*DR*: 111), she gives her a 'warm motherly salute' (113) and promises to be 'exactly as a mother to you' (118). But in Freudian terms it is precisely to the pre-oedipal stage of erotic attraction to the mother to which lesbianism reverts. Miss Aldclyffe can therefore be seen as Cytherea's 'mother's rival' in this sense as well. Whether or not Hardy 'knew what he was doing', the text is highly charged with eroticism, raising the interest and curiosity of the voyeur-reader by its very reluctance to comment explicitly on what it depicts (Bayley, 1978: 133–5).

The meeting between Cytherea and Miss Aldclyffe, her prospective employer, like that between the young lovers in the boat, is described in visual detail. It too takes place in the 'warm tint' of the afternoon sun, refracted through the crimson curtains and reflected from the wallpaper and carpets of a hotel room, investing the mistress with a 'burning glow' and bestowing upon the maid an 'orange light' which adds a 'voluptuousness' not ordinarily present in her face. It also brings out 'much of the youthful richness' in the older woman's 'decaying complexion' (DR: 87). The narrative dwells on the 'masculine cast' of Miss Aldclyffe's jaw, its 'Roman nose' and the 'prominent chin with which the Caesars are represented in ancient marbles' (88) in contrast with the girl's coquettish charms, especially in the moment when she turns like the girl in Greuze's painting. The two women thus appear to each other as objects of art as well as desire.

Cytherea's attentions to Miss Aldclyffe are also described in luxuriant detail, from the removing of dresses and stockings to the arranging and letting fall of the hair about the shoulders. The maid too has her expectations, which are slightly disappointed on discovering her new mistress 'harder and less warm' in her beauty than she had seemed on their first encounter, even if her hair 'proved to be all real; a satisfaction' (100–1). Miss Aldclyffe gains added mystery and interest by possessing a miniature of her father, but Cytherea soon finds that 'the woman of her romantic wanderings' has a savage temper, which is exacerbated by her awareness that she has taken on a new maid without references 'all because of her good l—' (106). Miss Aldclyffe's unwillingness to complete the word underlines her guilty awareness of a sexual component in her affection, a love which at this Victorian juncture dared not speak its name.

The key episode in the relationship between Cytherea and her mistress is, of course, the bedroom scene, which begins with Cytherea checking 'the reflection of her own magnificent resources in face and bosom' in the mirror, comforting herself and reaffirming her sense of identity after the row with her mistress. 'In bed and in the dark', however, 'Miss Aldclyffe haunted her mind more persistently than ever' as she 'called up starry visions of the

possible past of this queenly lady' (110–21). When her mistress
appears in person at her door, pleading to be let in, the restraints
of rank evaporate: 'It was mistress and maid no longer; woman
and woman only'. Other inhibitions also vanish:

> The instant they were in bed Miss Aldclyffe freed herself from
> the last remnant of restraint. She flung her arms round the
> young girl and pressed her gently to her heart.
> 'Now kiss me,' she said. 'You seem as if you were my own,
> own child!' (112)

Again, to call this intensity of feeling maternal is not to say that it
is altogether innocent.

Miss Aldclyffe's sexual possessiveness shows itself quite clearly
in her resentment that Cytherea should have allowed the lips she
has been 'sipping' like 'honey' to have been 'sullied' by male
contact. These attentions, it is stressed, are 'not of the kind that
Cytherea's instincts desired', being 'somewhat too rank and
sensuous' (116), though 'sensuous' was toned down to 'capricious'
in 1896, just as the servants' lack of suspicion of a 'carnal plot' (146)
was removed in the later edition. It is also made clear by Miss
Aldclyffe's insistence that she will not forget her 'as men do' but
be 'exactly as a mother' to her, and in the calm which comes to the
older woman once Cytherea has put her hair round her 'mamma's'
neck and given her 'one good long kiss', that the emotional need is
on the mistress's side, 'as if the maiden at her side afforded her a
protection against dangers which had menaced her for years'
(119). These dangers are unspecified but clearly sexual in nature,
affecting her very identity, making her 'changeable . . . like a
fountain, always herself, yet always another' (145).

Cytherea's sexual identity, however, is never seriously
threatened by her mistress's 'doting fondness'. She herself
remains as artless 'as was compatible with the complexity necessary to produce the due charm of womanhood' (145), a narrative
nudge in the direction of the voyeur-reader, reassuring him that
the main object of his erotic interest remains 'normal'. Any doubts
that the male reader may still entertain are soon put to rest by her
encounter with Miss Aldclyffe's mysterious steward, Aeneas Manston, who first appears to her distant gaze as an unidentified man,
'dark in outline' and 'of towering height', clearly built for
romance. His eyes are penetrative – she feels them 'going through

me' – and his voice 'masculine'. Even the way he subscribes to her
charity excites her: 'The soft tips of his fingers brushed the palm of
her glove as he placed the money within it'. The mere touching of
her clothes with those of this 'mysterious stranger' sends a 'thrill
through her whole body' (162–4).

The erotic atmosphere of the novel grows even more humid as
Manston takes advantage of a storm, whose outer raging acts as a
clear index of Cytherea's inner turmoil, to impress her with the
power of his organ (music throughout Hardy's work acting as a
metaphor for sexual attraction). His reverberating tones cut
through her surface personality, stirring hidden depths of passion: they 'shook and bent her to themselves, as a gushing brook
shakes and bends a shadow across its surface.' She finds herself
literally speechless, reduced to a silent admiring gaze, 'looking
with parted lips at his face' (167–8). Her sense of identity, the
stable image she had of herself as a coherent personality, has been
shattered.

A second erotic encounter with Manston takes place by a stream
where water once more gurgles metaphorically down from a
millpond 'to a lower level, under the cloak of rank, broad leaves –
the sensuous natures of the vegetable world'. The sun again serves
to light up the lovers in a 'purple haze'. Once more their clothes
touch, and this time he actually takes her hand. She fancies that
she can actually hear the shriek of the mandrakes, significantly
aphrodisiac plants, and is unable to withdraw her hand: 'She felt
as one in a boat without oars, drifting with closed eyes down a
river – she knew not whither' (252). The image, as in the opening
scene with Springrove, draws attention to the uncontrollability of
her passions. Her fear of Manston's power over her surfaces in a
strange sadomasochistic dream in which she is 'whipped with
dry bones suspended on strings, which rattled at every blow like
those of a malefactor on a gibbet', while Manston, or a form like
his, appears as the masked executioner (263–4).

The important feature of this dream, as of the whole relationship, is the masking of identity. Manston, like his mother (for it
turns out that she is Miss Aldclyffe), has a number of dark secrets
to conceal, including the murder of his wife and the attempt to
pass off his mistress in her place. Cytherea is finally rescued from
his grasp, returning to her first love, but too much has happened
for her to resume the serene mask of her youth convincingly. It is
not, as Lawrence complained, that she is not a 'real person'

(Lawrence, 1978: 435); it is the liberal humanist notion of stable personality that has been questioned. And while it would be wrong to claim too much for this mechanically plotted, melodramatic novel (not all incoherence is profound, nor all clumsy characterisation a subversion of liberal humanist ideology), it is only fair to recognise the extent to which it raises, whether consciously or unconsciously, important questions about women and their sexual identity.

## UNDER THE GREENWOOD TREE

A number of Hardy's early heroines are left mysterious not so much to question and explore their sexual identity as to endow them with an enigmatic quality which contributes to their erotic attraction. It is precisely because their image cannot be fixed that it fascinates. Fancy Day, for example, whose very name connotes her bright and airy charm, first appears as the absent owner of a 'small, light, and prettily shaped' boot, which, as the 'interesting receptacle of the little unknown's foot', leads the assembled members of the village choir to speculate on her beautiful face and enigmatic character (*UGT*: 45–6). What Barthes called the 'hermeneutic code' comes quickly into operation, arousing in male readers especially, a curiosity to know more about her, to solve the riddle of her personality and to pierce the secrets of her heart.

The much-discussed face soon makes itself visible, bestowing upon the carol singers a rare but welcome treat, when a blind from the window above the school suddenly opens,

> revealing to thirty concentrated eyes a young girl framed as a picture by the window architrave, and unconsciously illuminating her countenance to a vivid brightness by a candle she held in her left hand, close to her face, her right hand being extended to the side of the window. She was wrapped in a white robe of some kind, whilst down her shoulders fell a twining profusion of marvellously rich hair, in a wild disorder which proclaimed it to be only during the invisible hours of the night that such a condition was discoverable. Her bright eyes were looking into the grey world outside with an uncertain expression . . . (55)

This description, more like that of a painting than of a person, combines realistic detail with an additional element of mystery. The 'white robe of some kind', far from being an example of narrative carelessness, reflects an uncertainty in the observers as well as the observed, while the fact that her unrestrained luxuriance of hair is normally 'invisible' underlines the richness and rarity of the choir's erotic experience.

This 'vision' excites Dick Dewy and makes his 'body and soul tingle with novel sensations' when she enters the church the following morning. The scene becomes etched permanently in the young man's mind down to the last details of visual association, which tend to dominate, we are told, 'when reason is only exercising its lowest activity through the eye' (63–4). The narrator also enjoys dwelling on the details of Fancy's appearance at the dance organised by Dick's father, when her dark eyes with their curved brows, like 'two slurs in music', sparkle with 'a certain coquettishness' over her well-shaped nose, a genuine rarity in a world where 'there are a hundred pretty mouths and eyes for one pretty nose' (71). The narrator clearly poses as a connoisseur of female beauty and a sympathiser therefore with Dick's growing excitement. The young man is even allowed to progress from sight to touch, holding her so close that he feels 'her breath curling round his neck' (76). She becomes 'touchable, squeezable – even kissable' for the one evening (81), a momentary lapse in her normal unattainability and distance which has the effect of tantalising him still further.

The poor infatuated young man is driven into romantic agonies of doubt over Fancy's real feelings and intentions as the text poses more questions belonging to the hermeneutic code. Does she blush, Dick wonders, when he finally manufactures an encounter in front of the school? 'It was a question meditated several hundreds of times by her visitor in after-hours' and never resolved (84). He contrives more meetings at which she evinces obvious pleasure, but whether this is 'exultation at the hope her exceeding fairness inspired . . . or . . . true feeling . . . he could not anyhow decide' (87). 'I can't onriddle her, nohow,' says one of the locals (108) and this, of course, is part of her attraction. 'Was she a coquette?' asks Dick, pondering the number of times 'she had let him put her hand upon hers' during their dangerous game at her father's table and while washing in the same basin (123). 'What was the meaning of that speech?' he asks his father, recounting her prolonged silence when pressed to say if she cared for him, a silence broken only by the enigmatic answer 'that she didn't know' (125). Again, 'did she mean anything by her bearing towards him, or did she not?' (128). The questions hammer home both the urgency of his desire and the elusive nature of its object. This enigmatic 'bunch of sweets', an amalgam of all the qualities he admires, clear eyes, graceful neck, wavy hair, dainty little feet under a skirt full of 'pretty devices' (the artificial mingling with the 'natural' to create a delicacy Dick longs to consume), is momentarily 'captured and made a prisoner' when he gives her a lift in his wagon. She admits 'perhaps' to loving him 'a little' (131–4), only for him to press home his advantage when they stop at an inn. He asks her to marry him, looking 'expectantly at the ripe tint of her delicate mouth, waiting for what was coming forth'. Her lips gain in erotic attraction for being the source of the solution to his question. He does not, of course, pay any attention to what she actually says and ignores altogether her prohibition on kissing. The episode, once more, is subjected to erotic defamiliarisation as they emerge after half an hour: 'if Fancy's lips had been real cherries probably Dick's would have appeared deeply stained' (139). The comparison with cherries, conventional though it is, reinforces the notion of her as an object for male consumption.

Dick is kept a little longer in suspense by the attentions Fancy pays to Farmer Shiner and left totally in the dark about her temporary acceptance of the vicar's proposal, 'a secret', we are told in the final words of the novel, 'she would never tell' (208). There is, then, an ironic twist at the end even of this relatively light-hearted novel, for the enigmatic qualities which make Fancy Day such an alluring object of erotic fascination are irretrievably connected with a secretiveness which will make her a dangerous wife. In Lawrence's view, Fancy will remain dissatisfied while 'Dick will probably have a bad time of it' (Lawrence, 1978: 412). But, to use the dominant food metaphor of the novel, men cannot have their cake and eat it. They cannot securely possess what remains attractive only by being uncertain and mysterious.

## *A PAIR OF BLUE EYES*

If *Under the Greenwood Tree* celebrates the delights of the erotic, *A Pair of Blue Eyes* stresses its dangers. It is not the blue eyes themselves but the false visions they provoke which are at issue as Elfride Swancourt becomes the victim of her lovers' investment of her visual image with their own particular needs. They are all seen

. to paint Lacanian pictures of desire, to dream erotic dreams, to fix
her as a static object for their contemplation. The very location of
the action, according to the 1895 Preface, is a place 'pre-eminently
(for one person at least) the region of dream and mystery' (*PBE*:
35), the site of Hardy's courtship of his first wife. This particular
erotic dream, however, is to end in nightmare.

Elfride is introduced as a beautiful work of art, a combination of
the 'thoughtfulness of the Madonna della Sedia', the beautiful
figures 'of Rubens, without their insistent fleshiness' and the
'female faces of Correggio' (39–40). She first appears to the young
architect Stephen Smith 'in the prettiest of feminine guises, that is
to say, in demi-toilette, with plenty of loose hair tumbling down
about her shoulders' (47), but the image of her that fixes itself in
the 'pages of his memory', the 'table of his fancy', is that of her
singing about the frailty of love. The emphasis throughout is on
the visual impact of her beauty on his erotic gaze:

> Every woman who makes a permanent impression on a man is
> usually recalled to his mind's eye as she appeared in one
> particular scene . . . Miss Elfride's image chose the form in
> which she was beheld during these minutes of singing for her
> permanent attitude of visitation to Stephen's eyes during his
> sleeping and waking hours in after days. The profile is seen of a
> young woman in a pale grey silk dress with trimmings of swan's
> down, and opening up from a point in front, like a waistcoat
> without a shirt; the cool colour contrasting admirably with the
> warm bloom of her neck and face. The furthermost candle on the
> piano comes immediately in a line with her head, and half
> invisible itself, forms the accidentally frizzled hair into a nebu-
> lous haze of light, surrounding her like an aureola. Her hands
> are in their place on the keys, her lips parted, and trilling
> forth . . . Her head is forward a little, and her eyes directed
> keenly upward to the top of the page of music confronting her.
> (54–5)

It reads like a description of a painting or the instructions to an
illustrator, and Stephen falls in love with this mental picture rather
than with any 'essential' person. For a while his whole world is lit
up with Virgil's 'purple light' (62), but after their abortive elopement (she compromises herself by travelling with him from
Plymouth to Paddington only for her nerve to fail on arrival,

compelling her to take the return train back) she loses her
radiance in his eyes.

The pattern of illusion and disillusion is repeated in Elfride's
relations with Henry Knight, the fastidious London barrister and
man of letters who has an erotic vision of her in the evening
sun:

> Knight could not help looking at her. The sun was within ten
> degrees of the horizon, and its warm light flooded her face and
> heightened the bright rose colour of her cheeks to a vermilion
> red, their moderate pink hue being only seen in its natural
> tone where the cheek curved round into shadow. The ends of
> her hanging hair softly dragged themselves backwards and
> forwards upon her shoulders as each faint breeze thrust against
> or relinquished it. Fringes and ribbons of her dress, moved by
> the same breeze, licked like tongues upon the parts around
> them, and fluttering forward from shady folds caught likewise
> their share of the lustrous orange glow. (189)

The 'lustrous glow' is clearly a reflection of a lustful glance
longing to emulate those ribbons – Elfride could be called the
most lickable of Hardy's heroines – but it belongs more to the
narrator than to Knight, who is himself lit up in her eyes by the
sun streaming through the east window of her father's parish
church, shedding the 'same mellow lustre' (208).

Knight's problem is that he is shamefully slow to be aroused. It
takes a clifftop rescue in which she creates a rope from her
underclothes and allows herself to be so drenched with rain that
her 'diaphanous exterior robe' is made 'to cling to her like a
glove' (245–7) to make him fully aware of her body. He has been
seen as a precursor of Angel Clare, another example of Freud's
'abstinent young savant' who suffers from the repression of
sexuality required of a civilised society, sublimating his libidinal
energy to 'higher' cultural ends (Sumner, 1981: 122). But he is not
the only one to suffer for such repression. His 'romantic vision'
of Elfride, as well as being disembodied, is curiously 'coercive'
(Lucas, 1977:136). When he gives her a pair of earrings, he holds
her over a pool so that she can see herself as he sees her ('you
look shinier than ever,' he tells her). But then he blames her for
being 'so fond of finery' and fails to see the significance of the
words that slip from her when she flings away her face to avoid

his kiss: 'I lost the other earring doing like this' (*PBE*: 302–3). There is a self-evident gap between what he sees and what she is.

The coercive element in Knight's image of Elfride becomes increasingly clear. So high are his expectations, so strong his disapproval of all weakness, that he forces her into playing a false role, creating a different person: 'Elfride, under Knight's kiss, had certainly been a very different woman from herself under Stephen's' (329). The notion of these men refashioning her *under* their kisses is quite horrifying. But Knight then has the temerity to chastise her for his illusions. Catching her looking 'long and attentively' at herself in a mirror (355), presumably attempting to recover a sense of identity and to see herself as she is seen, he is far from being pleased. 'I looked into your eyes,' he complains, 'and thought I saw there truth and innocence as pure and perfect as ever embodied by God in the flesh of woman' (356). He demands to know the 'truth' about her and is, of course, bitterly disappointed when she tells him. Elfride, in the end, marries neither Knight nor Smith but Lord Luxellian, leaving the two disappointed rivals to travel in the same train with what they discover to be her dead body. Each characteristically blames himself for her death, which is in fact the result of a miscarriage. But they are to blame for some of her misfortunes; the novel anticipates *Tess* in showing 'how male visions of a woman corrupt, compromise and finally destroy her' (Lucas, 1977: 127).

These early novels, then, are full of visual pictures of women, detailed descriptions of their physical attractions and the effect they have upon male observers. Little attention is paid to the women as subjects, to their inner consciousness. Neither the men portrayed in these novels nor the narrator have much interest in what the objects of their desire think or feel. At times these novels seem to undermine the very notion of stable personality as their heroines are torn between sexual drives that they cannot control and coercive images from which they cannot escape. This question of identity, of women's self-understanding as subjects, as we shall see, becomes a dominant theme in the later novels.

# 4
# Women as Subjects: Romances and Fantasies

The novels of Hardy's middle period, from *Far from the Madding Crowd* to *Two on a Tower*, contain only two of the group gathered together under the title of 'Romances and Fantasies' in the Wessex Edition (*Two on a Tower* itself and *The Trumpet-Major*). Nevertheless the description in some ways fits all the novels of this period, since they are all concerned with the difference between subjective consciousness and objective reality. They are romances, plotted around a central love story, but they are also fantasies, exploring the extravagant dreams and unfulfilled desires of their protagonists. They continue to present women as objects of male fascination, dwelling on their visual charms as the screen on which erotic fantasy can play. But from Bathsheba Everdene onwards Hardy's heroines are not content simply to remain passive. They actively enjoy exploiting their charms, increasing the element of mystery which they recognise to be part of their fascination, exercising power and control over their male victims. Ethelberta Petherwin uses her beauty unashamedly to climb the social ladder, while Paula Power positively toys with her suitors.

These novels also explore female desire rather more fully, presenting women as subjects in this sense, suffering from libidinal drives which remain outside their control and beyond the accepted limits of their society. Eustacia Vye and Viviette Constantine struggle against these limits, challenging the conventionally passive role of women. They are perhaps too fantastic as characters to attain the tragic status of some of Hardy's later heroines, but the sexual and political tensions caused by their emotional demands give rise to an increased intensity of feeling, a greater seriousness, in these novels than in Hardy's earlier work.

49

## FAR FROM THE MADDING CROWD

The secret of a romantic heroine, as we have seen, is an element of elusiveness and mystery, both of which surround Bathsheba Everdene, who is first observed in secret like her biblical name-sake, the inspirer of David's love (2 Samuel 11: 2). Oak sees her on four separate occasions, in four different pictures. In the first she is seated in a wagon on a sunny spring morning smiling to herself in a small looking-glass and then blushing at her own reflection. Why she should do so is itself presented as a mystery:

> What possessed her to indulge in such a performance in the sight of the sparrows, blackbirds, and unperceived farmer who were alone its spectators, – whether the smile began as a factitious one, to test her capacity in that art, – nobody knows. (*FMC*: 44)

Remarking that the unusual setting, out of doors, lent 'novelty', that essential requisite of the erotic, to an otherwise familiar sight, the narrator suggests 'Woman's prescriptive infirmity' as the probable motive, postulating visions of future romantic triumphs. Oak himself, in what has been seen as a cliché designed to quench his erotic excitement (Poole, 1981: 329), pronounces his similar verdict: 'Vanity' (*FMC*: 44–5). That his judgement is not unimpaired by emotion is apparent from the second time he sees her, peeping through the crevices of the cow-shed roof. All he can see from his angle is that she is 'apparently young and graceful'. But since we all 'colour and mould according to the wants within us whatever our eyes bring in' and since he has 'for some time known the want of a satisfactory form to fill an increasing void within him . . . he painted her a beauty' (51–2). The picture he sees, in other words, owes as much to his desire as to her reality.

Oak's third vision of Bathsheba as 'A Girl on Horseback', a chapter title which could again be the title of a painting, is from the other side of a hedge, when she soon dismounts to present a tantalising picture, milk-pail in hand, with just enough of her left arm 'being shown bare to make Oak wish that the event had happened in summer, when the whole would have been revealed'. He certainly drinks his fill of 'the portrait she now presented him with', looking 'at her proportions with a long consciousness of pleasure' and deducing from 'the contours of her figure' that 'she must have had a beautiful neck and shoulders', secret though these have been kept 'since her infancy'. Such is the strength of Gabriel's erotic gaze that Bathsheba seems to feel the 'rays of male vision' emanating from him, 'conning' the 'page' of her face and form (54–5). Meeting for a fourth time when Oak awakes in his smoke-filled hut to find his head on her lap and her fingers unbuttoning his collar, she tantalises him in a different way by withholding her identity: '"Now find out my name," she said teasingly; and withdrew' (60). The absence caused by her departure to take over her inheritance causes him to 'idealize the removed object' still further and confirms his subjugation to her image.

It is not just Oak, of course, over whom Bathsheba exercises an erotic fascination. One of her employees describes in glowing terms how she appeared to him one day after riding, when 'her colours were up and her breath rather quick, so that her bosom plimmed and fell – plimmed and fell – every time plain to my eye' (387). The dialect adds just that touch of strangeness to the familiar appeal to the eyes. She is certainly the centre of attention among the farmers at the Corn Exchange:

> Something in the exact arch of her upper unbroken row of teeth, and in the keenly pointed corners of her red mouth when, with parted lips, she somewhat defiantly turned up her face to argue a point with a tall man, suggested that there was potentiality enough in that lithe slip of humanity for alarming exploits of sex, and daring enough to carry them out. (124)

This suggestion of sexual daring must, of course, come from the mind of a male observer. One of the farmers, Boldwood, presents a particularly easy victim, his ripeness for an 'ideal passion' being provoked by her anonymous Valentine, into which he reads answers to all his emotional needs. A series of questions, as he gazes at her card, underlines the erotic fascination of enigma:

> The mysterious influences of night invested the writing with the presence of the unknown writer. Somebody's – some *woman's* – hand had travelled softly over the paper bearing his name; her unrevealed eyes had watched every curve as she formed it; her brain had seen him in imagination the while.

Why should she have imagined him? Her mouth – were the lips red or pale, plump or creased? – had curved itself to a certain expression as the pen went on – the corners had moved with all their natural tremulousness: what had been the expression? (133)

The sender of the Valentine remains a 'misty shape' for him, taking 'form' only in his dreams.

Creative as he is in reading meaning and presence into this slight text, Boldwood cannot, in fact, interpret the signs emanating from Bathsheba as she helps Oak with the lambs:

> Perhaps in her manner there were signs that she wished to see him – perhaps not – he could not read a woman. The cabala of this erotic philosophy seemed to consist of the subtlest meanings expressed in misleading ways. Every turn, look, word, and accent contained a mystery quite distinct from its obvious import and not one had ever been pondered by him until now. (155)

There is, then, a semiotics of love as of every other human activity, an 'erotics' to which Oak is as sensitive as he is to the natural signs of forthcoming storms. He notices, for example, the small attentions Boldwood pays to Bathsheba during the Harvest Supper, actions which assume erotic significance only within an elaborate code of accepted behaviour: 'The meaning lay in the difference between actions none of which had any meaning of itself; and the necessity of being jealous . . . did not lead Oak to underestimate these signs' (189). Oak himself is likened to Eros in the famous scene in which he clasps her hands in an attempt to control her manipulation of the shears, winning only a rebuke both for this and for his temerity in criticising her behaviour towards Boldwood. Bathsheba, of course, remains a picture throughout this scene, especially when her face colours 'the angry crimson of a Danby sunset' (166), the narrative dwelling on the erotic effect of her blushing rather than its internal cause, her feelings.

Boldwood's misreading of Bathsheba stems in part from the fact that he spends so little time with her, producing those 'great aids to idealization in love . . . occasional observation of her from a distance, and the absence of social intercourse with her – visual familiarity, oral strangeness'. The 'smaller human elements . . . the pettinesses that enter so largely into all earthly living' are thus kept out of sight, allowing the object of his desire to take on 'a mild sort of apotheosis' (157). He is so unfamiliar with women as a species, who have hitherto been 'remote phenomena', that he stares at her 'blindly at gaze', unable even to resolve the hermeneutic question, 'Was she really beautiful?' (149–50). His anxiety mounts with his desire, the strength of his neurosis matching the intensity of the impulses repressed (Sumner, 1981: 49). His obsession with Bathsheba goes beyond the 'normal' processes of idealisation, becoming pathological, driving out all other interests and resulting finally in the murder of his rival. Among the evidence which permits his acquittal on the grounds of diminished responsibility are the wardrobes full of dresses labelled 'Bathsheba Boldwood' (*FMC*: 407). His desire, failing to secure a real object, fixes instead on fetishes which represent it.

Bathsheba, however, is the subject as well as the object of desire. She too has a romantic vision of the dashing Sergeant Troy lit up by his lantern when first they become entangled (193). A walking symbol of male potency, he is forever 'whirling his crop' (202) and flashing his sword. His exhibition in 'The Hollow amid the Ferns', an obviously symbolic landscape for the dexterous exercise of his weapon, leaves Bathsheba 'aflame to the very hollows of her feet', feeling 'like one who had sinned a great sin' (218). Her sense of guilt, Lawrence complained, soon overcomes her first sexual excitement (Lawrence, 1978: 219, 413), while her hysterical reaction to seeing Troy kiss the dead body of Fanny Robin and the 'moral masochism' of her self-condemnation for her treatment of Boldwood have been taken as further evidence of repression on her part, a profound regret for the loss of her innocence (Kramer, 1979: 64). For Bathsheba, then, as for Boldwood, the erotic and the sexual are very different. To be infatuated by visual charms and to indulge in erotic fantasy is quite consistent with severe sexual repression.

Bathsheba's eventual acceptance of Gabriel, likened by Lawrence to 'a dog that watches the bone and bides the time' (Lawrence, 1978: 413), involves an attempt to place strict limits on the play of fancy, 'the romance growing up in the interstices of a mass of hard prosaic reality', such 'good fellowship' as they share being founded on a knowledge of the worst (*FMC*: 419). It is difficult not to think of Bathsheba's father, who in order to introduce erotic novelty into his marriage and to enjoy Foucault's game of defying the law used to call his wife by her maiden name and make her take off her wedding ring so that 'he could thoroughly fancy he was doing wrong and committing the seventh' (97). And it is hard to believe his daughter will deny herself for ever the delusions and delights of the erotic. For there is little evidence of any change in her attitudes while Oak even asks her to dress her hair as she had worn it when he first saw her, so that 'she seemed in his eyes remarkably like the girl of that fascinating dream' (423). He clearly needs to retain that image even within marriage.

There is, of course, a political dimension to Bathsheba's struggles to assert herself. Her power over men is linked to the erotic fascination she exerts over them. Once this is diminished she can be controlled, just as Troy subdues his horses and Oak his ewes (Boumelha, 1982: 33). She is one more 'mettlesome' beast that needs to be 'put through its paces' (Poole, 1981: 332). When her attempts to run her own farm begin to founder she is forced to plead women's weakness in order to regain Oak's services. But even in apologising to Boldwood for her 'wicked' behaviour, she propounds the power-ful feminist argument that it 'is difficult for a woman to define her feelings in language which is chiefly made by men to express theirs' (*FMC*: 376). The novel does not pursue the matter further. Bath-sheba's failures, both private and public, reduce her to reliance upon her sturdy male Oak. Questions have nevertheless been raised about the role of women which Hardy's later work will press still further.

## THE HAND OF ETHELBERTA

There is a political element too in Hardy's next novel, in which the heroine gains social status, marrying into the aristocracy, at the expense of her emotional integrity. Taking advantage of men's fascination with her physical appearance, she exploits the ambi-guity and mystery with which they surround her both to cover over the secret of her origins and to manipulate a number of them to the point of proposal. These men are more ridiculous than she is, dominated as they are by the lust of their eyes. But she herself achieves in marriage a mixed blessing, being lumbered with a lecherous old lord, while her sister, content to remain within her own class and to limit her aspirations to one true love, is rewarded with the hand they would both have preferred.

Ethelberta Petherwin is introduced at the beginning of the novel in familiar glowing terms, stepping into the evening sunlight for a country walk to the delight of her male observers. 'Dang me! if she isn't a pretty piece,' exclaims the milkman, immediately indulging in erotic fantasy: 'A man could make a meal between them eyes and chin' (*HE*: 34). He and the hostler discuss her attributes at some length with similarly unsubtle innuendo – a rural form of defamiliarisation. Even the ground on which she walks proclaims her an object of erotic fascination, responding to the impress of her feet with the 'sound of quick kisses' (38).

Christopher Julian, who meets Ethelberta on her walk, cannot remove his eyes from her, 'keeping them fixed with mathematical exactness upon one point in her face' (40) while she, making the most of her enigmatic charm, 'smiled a smile of many meanings' (41). When he plays the music at a dance she attends, he 'gave himself up with a curious and far from unalloyed pleasure to the occupation of watching Ethelberta' (63), an activity shared by most of the male characters in the novel. She rewards him once more with an enigmatic and undefinable look, 'the well-known spark of light upon the well-known depths of mystery' (64). Similarly, when he visits her in London, she remains unreadable in her response: 'she might or might not have been said to blush' (138), in contrast with her younger sister, Picotee, who is forever revealing her feelings through her cheeks and makes no secret of her love for the young musician. Ethelberta's game, however, is seen to be dangerous. Christopher expresses his fear that to 'disentangle' her 'mystery' would be to discover indifference (142). He even finds himself on one occasion kissing the wrong sister without for a while noticing the difference. The object of his desire, in other words, as will become apparent at the end of the novel, is not that firmly fixed.

The reader, of course, has privileged access to the secrets of both sisters' hearts, having been shown Ethelberta in her room at 'that dreamy period . . . when ladies' fancies, having been shut up close as their fans during the day, begin to assert themselves anew'. She celebrates her release from the repression required by society by walking up and down, curling 'her pretty nether lip within her pretty upper one a great many times' and gazing at 'a picture within her mind' (45). Picotee too has been observed by a group of London sportsmen who enjoy the picturesque spectacle of 'woman's endurance and patience under neglect' as she waits in the rain in the hope of meeting Mr Julian at the point where they usually pass. She becomes the subject of their idle speculation, the focus of enigmatic and erotic interest, as they ask a number of questions about her motives (57). But it is only the older sister who knows how to use such mystery to her advantage, her fashionable verses presenting 'a series of playful defences of the supposed strategy of womankind in fascination, courtship, and marriage' (47–8). She has to instruct the innocent Picotee on the importance of keeping her love secret. The man must never know what she feels for him: 'He must think it only. The difference between his thinking and knowing is often the difference between your winning and losing' (72).

Ethelberta puts her principles so effectively into practice that she soon has a number of eligible bachelors hot in her pursuit: the painter Ladywell, the landowner Neigh, who gazes at her photograph 'with a face of cynical adoration' (164), and the most valuable prize of all, the aging but wealthy Lord Mountclere. Humiliated by being discovered checking the extent of Neigh's land, she swears never to marry him: 'He is one of those horrid men who love with their eyes, the remainder part of him objecting all the time to the feeling.' But Picotee points out that Lord Mountclere is even worse: 'I never saw anything like the look of his eyes upon you' (241). He turns out to be dominated by the scopic drive, deriving erotic pleasure from flicking through the pages of a fashion magazine and 'scrutinizing the faces of the women one by one' (261).

Ethelberta, however, is flattered by Lord Mountclere's attentions. He chases her across the Channel in order to share her railway carriage to Rouen, 'overtly observing' her even while she is awake (267) but increasing his attention when she falls asleep:

> Wearied . . . she closed her eyes. And then her enamoured companion more widely opened his, and traced the beautiful features opposite him. The arch of the brows – like a slur in music – the drop of the lashes, the meeting of the lips, and the sweet rotundity of the chin – one by one and all together, they were adored, till his heart was like a retort full of spirits of wine. (270)

Intoxication may increase desire, but it reduces performance and the old man struggles significantly to reach the top of the cathedral spire at Rouen. Ethelberta encourages him all the time, urging him to climb 'through the fog to the sunshine', even lying about the number of steps to go, the metaphorical equivalent of feigned sexual excitement. When they finally reach the summit, of course, and Lord Mountclere sinks panting to the ground, there is nothing to be seen. 'We have lost our labour . . . after all,' Ethelberta is forced to admit (275–6). The disappointment of the sexual in comparison with the erotic has been made abundantly clear.

The narrative reaches its farcical climax when financial circumstances force Ethelberta to make a choice between her suitors. Her mother advises her strongly to 'warm up the best man of them again a bit' (273). All three of them converge upon her hotel in Rouen, where Ladywell and Neigh, crouched upon their respective balconies, overhear snatches of Lord Mountclere's proposal and her evasive reply. But she cannot remain enigmatic for ever and is forced to decide, encumbering herself for life with a man about whom she can have no illusions. Christopher Julian is horrified at the way 'the corners of his mouth twitched as the telegraph needles of a hundred little erotic messages from his heart to his brain'. He sees at once that Lord Mountclere is a lover of 'nymph-like shapes' rather than a respecter of persons (329–30) and that her choice of such a man for a husband must be completely cynical. Christopher turns his attention to the younger sister, who is thus rewarded for her loyalty in love, while Ethelberta is left with the products of artifice, wealth and art. No explicit moral is drawn, but the novel can be seen as a sustained if not altogether serious portrait of the difficulties and dangers involved in attempting to manipulate the flickering and inconstant world of the erotic.

## THE RETURN OF THE NATIVE

Most of the endings of the novels so far considered impose marriage, signifying harmony and wholeness, on fractured and confused relationships composed of illusory images. The impossibility of complete emotional satisfaction, the gap between infinite desire and its finite fulfilment, the tension between women seen as objects of erotic fantasy and their developing consciousness of themselves, partially opened in the text, is closed, or supposed to be closed, by these endings. This is not the case with *The Return of the Native*. The split within its heroine, Eustacia Vye, is never 'healed' or covered over. The complexity, even the confusion, of her characterisation is partly a result of constant textual revision, transforming her from a satanic antagonist to a romantic protagonist (Paterson, 1960: 29). But it is more importantly a product of the tension between her function as an erotic object and her emergence as a subject with disturbing desires of her own.

First glimpsed as a mysterious female silhouette on the horizon, 'The Figure Against the Sky', Eustacia is soon seen a little closer, lit up by the dying embers of a bonfire from which she extracts a disturbingly phallic stick with a 'live coal at its end'. This she proceeds to blow into renewed life, causing the 'momentary irradiation . . . of two matchless lips and a cheek' (*RN*: 83). The famous 'Queen of Night' chapter builds on this tantalising glimpse, but even here more is obscured than revealed by the portentous Paterian 'verbal decoration' with which she is depicted (Bayley, 1978: 70). Like earlier romantic heroines she exudes a sense of erotic mystery, enhanced by plentiful references to pagan goddesses. Her eyes are 'full of nocturnal mysteries' while her lips are a lecher's delight, beautiful and silent: 'The mouth seemed formed less to speak than to quiver, less to quiver than to kiss, some might have added, less to kiss than to curl.' She conjures up exotic images of 'Bourbon roses, rubies, and tropical delights', music and the motion of the sea (*RN*: 93–4).

As in the description of earlier heroines, a series of questions adds to the air of mystery: 'Why did a woman of this sort live on Egdon Heath?', 'Where did her dignity come from?' and 'Where was a mouth matching hers to be found?' (95–6). A false answer, in terms of Barthes' hermeneutic code, is supplied to this last question by her secret meeting with Wildeve. But she spurns his offer of a 'tame love' (109), rejecting also the reddleman's plea for her to leave him free to marry Thomasin 'with a laugh which unclosed her lips so that the sun shone into her mouth as into a tulip, and lent it a similar scarlet fire' (116). Even the sun, then, burns to penetrate the mystery of her sexuality.

All this fits the pattern of 'women seen' in Hardy's other novels. What is unusual about Eustacia, however, is the depth of her desire, 'deepened', we are told, by her lonely existence on Egdon Heath (96), that place of 'strange phantoms' and 'midnight dreams' which is 'untameable' and hostile to civilisation (35), a symbol of the unconscious and its terrifying fears and desires (Meisel, 1972: 74–5). Eustacia's longing for Wildeve is irrational,

uncontrollable and inconstant, fanned into life 'by his skill in
deserting her at the right moments'. The feeling she had 'idly
given' when he was readily available is 'dammed into a flood'
when he wants to marry Thomasin (*RN*: 120), the metaphor
suggesting the fluidity as well as the perversity of subconscious
desire. Later she falls in love with an image of Clym Yeobright
fashioned more from her needs than from his qualities. Having
spent an afternoon 'entrancing herself by imagining the fascination which must attend a man come direct from beautiful Paris
– laden with its atmosphere, familiar with its charms', she invests
the two words he speaks to her and the voice she overhears in
conversation with an inward passion reflected in her outward
features:

> All emotional things were possible to the speaker of that 'good
> night'. Eustacia's imagination supplied the rest. . . . She glowed;
> remembering the mendacity of the imagination she flagged; then
> she freshened; then she fired; then she cooled again. It was a cycle
> of aspects, produced by a cycle of visions. (141)

The nature of these visions, their uncovering of sexual desire, is
clearly indicated not only by her entering her house to discover
her grandfather 'enjoying himself over the fire, raking about the
ashes and exposing the red-hot surface of the turves, so that their
lurid glare irradiated the chimney-corner with the hues of a
furnace', but also by the complex but 'exciting dream' she has
that night, part of which is described in detail:

> She was dancing to wondrous music, and her partner was the
> man in silver armour who had accompanied her through the
> previous fantastic changes, the visor of his helmet being
> closed. The mazes of the dance were ecstatic. Soft whispering
> came into her ear from under the radiant helmet, and she felt
> like a woman in Paradise. Suddenly these two wheeled out
> from the mass of dancers, dived into one of the pools of the
> heath, and came out somewhere beneath into an iridescent
> hollow, arched with rainbows. 'It must be here,' said the voice
> by her side, and blushingly looking up she saw him removing
> his casque to kiss her. At that moment there was a cracking
> noise, and his figure fell into fragments like a pack of cards.
> She cried aloud, 'O that I had seen his face!'. (141–2)

It is an extraordinary dream, symbolising as it does the fall of man
(and woman) as a result of desire, which cannot be satisfied since
the image upon which it fixes fractures into fragments. What they
are seeking remains unspecified, capturing the vagueness and
fluidity of all dreams. She wakes up to repeat her wish, insisting
that the mysterious helmeted figure was 'meant for Mr. Yeobright'
(143).

The narrator seems at times to condemn Eustacia, observing
moralistically: 'The perfervid woman was by this time half in
love with a vision.' Her passion is described as 'fantastic', lowering her 'as an intellect'. But it raises her 'as a soul' (143), her
openness to these depths of feeling presumably lifting her
above those who achieve respectability through repression.
Lacking the opportunity 'for seeing and being seen' normally
provided by the church (145), she makes 'the sleaziest of bar-
gains' with the infatuated young Charley (Guerard, 1963: 65),
allowing him to hold her hand for a quarter of an hour if she
can take his part in the mumming and so come face to face
with the object of her desire. What she sees on this occasion
'riveted her gaze': a face described in terms of 'Rembrandt's
intensest manner', as mysterious as her own, neither conventionally handsome nor what is called 'thoughtful' but 'overlaid
with legible meanings', depicting among other things 'the
mutually destructive interdependence of spirit and flesh', the
'chaining' of 'deity' and infinite desire 'within an ephemeral
human carcase'. The effect upon her is 'palpable' (*RN*: 161–3).
She surrounds the object of her desire with an 'unreasonable
nimbus of romance' and becomes 'infatuated with a stranger'
(170).

Clym's vision of Eustacia is similarly distorted by desire. She
first appears to him in the 'fantastic guise' of the Turkish knight,
'only the sparkle of her eyes being visible between the ribbons
which covered her face' (166). She is likened to the 'mysterious
emanation', the Queen of Love, which appeared before Aeneas.
The effect upon Clym is equally mystifying, causing him to 'fall
into a reverie'. He stands 'gazing' at her figure, finally resolving
the enigma of her sex by asking her directly (166–9). She becomes
known to him as the anonymous enigmatic 'beauty on the hill'
(201) and he builds what his mother calls a 'castle in the air' (216),
the idea of marrying her and settling on Egdon, after only one
more meeting. When they do arrange regular meetings, one of

which is described in the ominously entitled chapter 'An Hour of Bliss and Many Hours of Sadness', it is significant that they rate words well below kisses. Even by the end of the chapter Clym is beginning to become 'accustomed to the first blinding halo kindled about him by love and beauty' and to realise how irreconcilable are the requirements of Eustacia, his mother and himself (223).

That their marriage will end in misery after 'consuming their mutual affections at a fearfully prodigal rate' (261) is inevitable, given the illusory images on which it is based and the extent of Clym's psychological problems: the unresolved Oedipus complex which prevents his accepting the need to leave his possessive mother and the severity of his superego, which makes unbearable demands upon his capacity for altruism and for work (Sumner, 1981: 110–13). The tragic end is hastened by Wildeve's revived passion for Eustacia, reawakened by the romantic inaccessibility she now acquires as another man's wife. The narrative mocks Wildeve as 'the Rousseau of Egdon', yearning for the unattainable while being 'weary of that offered', preferring the remote to the accessible (*RN*: 237). Eustacia herself finds repose only in death, when she presents a striking picture to the joint gaze of her male admirers. For now she seems whiter in complexion than ever before, 'her finely carved mouth' finally silenced, 'as if a sense of dignity had just compelled her to leave off speaking'. She is partly a work of art and partly a piece of nature, her black hair surrounding her brow 'like a forest'. She has 'found an artistically happy background' (393) but only by returning to the status of an object, all subjective longings having been extinguished.

At the end of the novel, Charley's devotion to Eustacia, 'a romantic and sweet vision' the inner details of whose life he can only conjecture (338), and Diggory Venn's dogged attachment to Thomasin seem to be applauded. Charley is rewarded with the gift of Eustacia's hair and Diggory with Thomasin's hand (in marriage). But a footnote warns discerning readers not to be content with this imposed ending: in 'the original conception of the story' Venn does not marry but disappears 'mysteriously' from the heath. 'Readers can therefore choose between the endings,' Hardy announces, recommending 'the more consistent conclusion', in other words the unhappy one (413). For there can be no happy ending, no complete satisfaction of desire, whose insatiable needs, fed by dreams and fostered by fantasy, cannot but find the 'real' world a pale shadow.

## THE TRUMPET-MAJOR

Written for an editor who wanted 'much honest love-making' and praised by a critic for its 'wholesome' qualities (Taylor, 1982: 79–82), with a heroine Hardy promised would be thoroughly 'good' (Millgate, 1971: 152), *The Trumpet-Major* sounds an unlikely source of eroticism. Yet its central subject, symbolised in the weather vane depicted in Hardy's own design on the cover of the first edition, could be said to be sexual inconstancy, the vagaries of desire, together with the difficulties and dangers of repression. The Lovedays' weather vane is described in the text as 'a revolving piece of statuary' on top of a pole, which 'had been a soldier in red before he became a sailor in blue', made in the likeness of John Loveday but then changed to that of his brother Bob. It could not be relied on to tell the direction of the wind because of the 'variable currents' caused by a neighbouring hill (*T-M*: 48). It can be taken as a Lacanian symbol of Anne Garland's desire, which seems to veer between the two brothers, or of Bob's inconstancy in love. Anne calls her mother a 'weathercock' when she changes her tune about Festus Dorriman, whom she first encourages as a suitor and then abandons (111). Nothing, it seems, is constant in the world of desire depicted in this novel.

For all its lightness of tone, *The Trumpet-Major* is quite cynical about sexual attraction. When Overcombe becomes the site of a military camp, we are told: 'Every belle in the village soon had a lover,' followed by those who 'scarcely deserved that title . . . many of the soldiers being not at all particular' in their taste. This 'large scale courtship' causes inevitable friction with the 'dispossessed young men' of the village (106). Anne Garland, who is besieged by three different suitors – a soldier, a sailor and a member of the yeomanry cavalry – can therefore be taken as typical. She is introduced on the opening page of the novel as typically enigmatic in appearance, her hair neither blonde nor brunette and her upper lip 'scarcely descending so far as it should' in the middle, giving her face an ambiguous unintended smile which 'some people' found 'very attractive' (39). She is shown to be diffident, even frightened, of men, preferring to remain at home rather than accompany her mother to the miller's party. Yet when her mother suggests they could indeed stay at home, uncertain of that too she 'abstractedly brought her hands together on her bosom, till her fingers met tip to tip' (57). The suggestion is not of primness and propriety, dullness and insipidity, of which so many critics have accused her, but of self-consciousness of her sexual attractiveness.

It is scarcely surprising that Anne should be aware of her attractions for the opposite sex, given the attentions men pay her. Festus Dorriman, who was 'early in love, and had . . . suffered from the ravages of that passion thirteen distinct times' (89), pounces on her first at the party and then on her way to deliver papers to his miserly uncle. Like Bathsheba Everdene, she can actually feel his lustful gaze: 'She knew that the bothering yeoman's eyes were travelling over her from his position behind, creeping over her shoulders, up to her head, and across her arms and hands' (92). In a series of farcical scenes he manages to get near enough to steal a kiss from her by feigning an apoplectic swoon while she, wriggling free from his embrace and loosening a plank on a bridge over which he pursues her, dampens his ardour in the river. She then blunts it when he traps her in a lonely cottage, escaping from a window while he breaks his symbolic sword 'between the joints of the shutters, in an attempt to rip them open'. She finally gallops away on his horse, leaving him 'brimful of suppressed passion' (238). For all the buffoonery, these events clearly symbolise the rape which is uppermost in Festus's mind.

John Loveday's courtship is somewhat more sedate. Anne, who is flattered by his attentions, sees him as 'a good and sincere fellow, for whom she had almost a sisterly feeling' (130). That he feels more for her is clear when she faints in his arms after escaping from the furious Festus. He holds her 'tenderly', looking down at her 'lashes lying upon each cheek' as they are lit up once more by the sun and at her loosened locks, 'usually as tight as springs' but now 'uncoiled by the wildness of her ride'. In an answering moment of release from repression and a 'state of ecstatic reverence', he kisses her (241–2). The trumpet-major, aware of her deeper feelings for his brother, is normally meticulous in his restraint, keeping his feelings 'religiously held in check' (308). 'Why don't he clipse her to his side, like a man?' ask the local lads as he walks 'about a yard from her right hand'. Even

Anne, angry at his brother's continuing inconstancy and eager therefore to encourage John, grows impatient at his refusal to take advantage of some stepping-stones to help her across, envying the companion of a young shepherd who has no such qualms. She offers him one more opportunity to hold her while she cleans her shoes, insisting that he tie her ribbons so that his fingers cannot avoid getting 'mixed with the curls of her forehead', sighing with frustration as he groans and trembles with suppressed emotion (316–20). The struggle continues with the virtuous man colouring whenever his 'sweet vision' appears but succeeding in such self-control that 'the blush of delight was at once mangled and slain'. Reminded of his earlier proposal, he can only stammer a reply in 'a dry, small, repressed voice' (322–3). The whole account is agonisingly erotic, arousing expectations which are continually disappointed.

Bob Loveday's remedy for desire is not restraint but indulgence, giving in to its frequent changes of direction and never brooding over disappointment, 'love being so much more effectually got rid of by displacement than by attempted annihilation' (191). Once again Hardy's language uncannily anticipates Freud. Bob deserts Anne first for an actress of dubious reputation and then for a young master-baker's daughter. 'You are too easily impressed by new faces,' she tells him (197) but always manages to forgive, her desire remaining fixed on its object. She is forever gazing at him from her window and when he erects an aeolian harp in the garden she interprets its sound: 'Remember me! think of me!' (194). She dresses in her prettiest jackets and boots in an attempt to prevent his joining the navy but although he acknowledges the erotic 'pleasure of sighting that young girl forty times a day, and letting her sight me' (275), he nevertheless departs.

Bob's playing with Anne's emotions continues on his return from the Napoleonic Wars, when he has little difficulty in recapturing her affections by dressing in his finest uniform and parading before her window, soon getting 'a rise to his bait' (328–9). The narrator too plays games with the reader's erotic interest, for a 'warm mysterious hand' squeezes Anne's in the dark, only to prove to be her mother's. She cannot, however, resist his embraces, at first protesting too much, 'I don't like you, Bob; I don't!', but ending in tears, 'the emotions which had been suppressed, bottled up, and concealed since Bob's return having made themselves a sluice at last' (332–4).

The narrative makes no attempt to conceal Anne's 'perverse desire for the less worthy' of the two brothers (338). Desire, it has shown, *is* perverse. For some it flits from one object to another, while for others it remains fixed on an object the conscious mind rejects. It cannot be repressed without terrible difficulty and suffering. Its medium is primarily visual, being provoked by the superficial attractions of pretty features and bright clothes and increased by the imagination dwelling on the mysterious and enigmatic. To follow its lead is to follow an inconstant weather vane. All these features of Hardy's tragic vision are present in this predominantly comic novel with its famous final paragraph in which the features of the trumpet-major, the one thoroughly 'good' character, flicker momentarily in the candlelight before he marches off into the night, to be 'silenced for ever upon one of the bloody battle-fields of Spain' (344). So much for wholesomeness and restraint.

## A LAODICEAN

*A Laodicean* marks a return to the erotic delights of speculation upon a mysterious beauty who exploits her enigmatic charms almost to her own cost. Paula Power, its lukewarm heroine, leads on the narrator as well as the characters, a postscript to the preface complaining that she 'tantalized the writer by eluding his grasp for some time' (*AL*: 34). She first appears, teetering on the verge of baptism by complete immersion, while George Somerset, a passing architect, peers in through a chapel window. His view, like Gabriel Oak's, is partial and limited: 'he could not see her face' but his 'imagination, stimulated by this beginning, set about filling in the meagre outline with most attractive details'. He is particularly taken with her hair, which 'threw off the lamp-light in a hazy lustre', and although none of her features are 'flawless, the nameless charm of them altogether was only another instance of how beautiful a woman can be as a whole' (46–7).

Setting himself to penetrate her mystery, Somerset speculates on her character from the evidence of her bedroom, in which he catches a fleeting glance of silk scarves and satin slippers (66–9). The landlord of his inn reveals that she and her friend Charlotte de Stancy are 'more like lovers than maid and maid', a tantalising snippet of information which he immediately qualifies by denying all knowledge of Paula's feelings, 'for she's as deep as the North Star' (79). She seems Laodicean or lukewarm in sex as well as religion (Millgate, 1971: 172), showing a 'curious coyness' about accompanying Somerset alone around the castle, but she is quite uninhibited with Charlotte, clasping her fingers behind her neck and smiling 'tenderly in her face'. Somerset, in his role of voyeur, watching unobserved and overhearing their conversation, finds this 'a very beautiful action', presumably because it arouses wishes of his own (*AL*: 108–10). Nevertheless she remains an enigma. 'So imaginative was his passion,' we are told, 'that he hardly knew a single feature of her countenance well enough to remember it in her absence' (115).

Paula clearly enjoys exercising the erotic power she wields over Somerset. She deliberately tantalises him, first by bending over him as he is sketching so that 'the breath of her words fanned his ear' (107) and then by asking him to teach her to feel the difference between early and late Gothic, which requires his guiding her ungloved fingers along the curves of an arch-mould with his own 'hot and trembling' hand. He is left to speculate on the motives behind the 'inscrutable seriousness with which she applied herself to his lesson', although the 'bottomless depth in her eyes' vouchsafes no answer. He ponders at some length whether her apparent 'imperception of his feeling' represents 'the very sublimity of maiden innocence' or not. 'If not,' he decides, 'the coquetry was no great sin' (117). The possibility of her being 'a finished coquette and dissembler' recurs to him when she manufactures another 'accidental' meeting. Part of her attraction for him, however, lies in his inability to answer these questions. 'Whatever she might be,' he concludes, 'she was not a creature starched very stiffly by Puritanism' (102). He clearly prefers her lukewarm, even blowing hot and cold, to frigid.

Paula remains a mystery to Somerset. She allows him to love her but not to kiss her (146). Even the villainous Dare and Havill, concealed observers of their tête-à-tête in a tent, find her feelings opaque: 'she did not satisfy curiosity as Somerset satisfied it; she piqued it'. While Somerset's infatuation is obvious, 'Paula remained an enigma all through the scene' (155). Dare tries to manipulate her charms to his advantage by arranging for his easily aroused father, Captain de Stancy, to observe her through a hole in her gymnasium wall. The result, as seen through the captain's eyes, is a 'sort of optical poem':

Paula, in a pink flannel costume, was bending, wheeling and undulating in the air like a gold-fish in its globe, sometimes ascending by her arms nearly to the lantern, then lowering herself till she swung level with the floor. . . . The white manilla ropes clung about the performer like snakes as she took her exercise, and the colour in her face deepened. (196–7)

The ropes here fulfil the same function as the ribbons in *A Pair of Blue Eyes*, symbolising the longings of the scopic drive. The captain's eyes, needless to say, remain 'glued' to the object of his gaze. To complete the picture and to fit in with the pattern observed in other descriptions of Hardy's women, the sun breaks through the gymnasium windows, 'irradiating her with a warm light that was incarnadined by her pink doublet and hose' (197). This warmth, of course, proceeds as much from the observer as from the sun. She becomes even redder when de Stancy, inserting a passage from *Romeo and Juliet* into a performance of *Love's Labour's Lost*, steals a kiss, described once more with momentarily defamiliarising circumlocution as a 'sweet and long-drawn osculation' (255). But she enters quite willingly, even 'mischievously', into an erotic game over a glass which they both touch with their lips (317–18) and eventually agrees to marry him after Somerset has been falsely represented as a gambler and sponger.

Paula's real feelings are made a mystery to the readers as well as to poor Somerset, whom she teases mercilessly in her letters from Europe while he remains in her castle, which keeps 'her image' ever 'before him' and in which there is 'no nook . . . to which he had not access' (282). He is shown reading 'the first letter he had ever received from her', which ponders the possibility of revealing what she feels:

Shall I tell you? No. For, if it is a great emotion, it may afford you a cruel satisfaction at finding I suffer through separation; and if it be a growing indifference to you, it will be inflicting gratuitous unhappiness upon you to say so, if you care for me; as I *sometimes* think you may do a *little*.

Here Somerset lets out an exasperated 'O, Paula', before reading her disarmingly frank analysis of the erotic delights of enigma: 'it is better that you should guess at what I feel than that you should distinctly know it'. For if she were to tell him what he wants, he would soon grow 'weary' of the news and lose the 'emotion' that he now enjoys. 'A woman who is *only* a creature of evasions and disguises', she admits, 'is very disagreeable' (283), which implies, as a later letter openly admits, 'I feel more than I say' (287). Somerset, who presses her to be more 'explicit' (284), argues, in anticipation of Derrida, that writing is more open to 'misunderstandings' than speech, 'for the eyes may reveal what the lips do not' (286). Even *their* meaning, however, cannot be fixed: 'You have always been ambiguous', he admits, and the 'encouragement' he read in her 'eyes' may not have extended to her heart (209).

Paula remains, in other words, a mystery, only marginally less open to misinterpretation in her presence than in her absence. And that, she realises, is the secret of her fascination. This, at least, is one interpretation of the ending of the novel, when all has been explained and she is safely married to Somerset. She surveys the smoking ruins of her castle, which has served throughout the novel as an extension of her personality. Its destruction seems to symbolise the breaking down of the defences which have allowed her to keep her distance and to retain her erotic attraction. For Somerset, like Clym Yeobright, has been building an erotic castle in the air. Little wonder, then, that she cannot help repressing a sigh as she utters her famous last line, 'I wish my castle wasn't burnt; and I wish you were a de Stancy!' (437). Neither wish can be fulfilled. It is one of the inevitable features of desire that it cannot be thoroughly satisfied. The supposedly happy ending of marriage actually involves the destruction of her illusions and of his.

## TWO ON A TOWER

*Two on a Tower* adds one more dimension to the portrait of women as subjects as well as objects of desire, decribing the infatuation of a mature woman for a younger man. The novel opens with the lonely Lady Viviette Constantine, abandoned by her explorer-husband, looking out over a sexually symbolic landscape dominated by a 'tower in the form of a classic column' which rises 'to a considerable height' over its surrounding firs (*TT*: 31). This phallic tower becomes the scene of her encounter with the young astronomer Swithin St Cleeve, whose youthful beauty and delicate complexion, reminiscent of Raphael, she cannot resist. He remains unconscious of her presence, his eyes fixed on the stars, while 'a warmer wave of her warm temperament glowed visibly through her' (35). Much is made of her 'soft dark eyes . . . the natural indices of a warm and affectionate, perhaps slightly voluptuous temperament, languishing for want of something to do, cherish, or suffer for' (49–50). The desire in this case lies all on the side of the lady rather than the poor man, whose beauty, following a familiar pattern, grows 'richer in her imagination than in the real' (53). She makes further moonlit visits to the tower, where the object of her gaze is clearly the astronomer rather than the stars. On one occasion, 'her eyes became so sentimentally fixed on his face that it seemed as if she could not withdraw them' (67). It is the visual image, once more, on which her desire becomes fixed, increasing as a result of his 'mental inaccessibility', his far greater interest in the heavens than in her (68). Her wooing gains in erotic interest for being secret, involving the cutting of a curl of his hair while he sleeps and the holding of his hands, even the bestowing of a kiss, as he lies on a sick-bed.

Swithin himself is painfully slow to be aroused, even to become aware of the nature of Viviette's interest in him. Summoned to her tower after his recovery, he sees her lit up for the first time in the erotic rays of the setting sun. But it requires his overhearing some rustic rumination on the lady's 'wrong desire' for him to reinterpret the looks and kisses she has given him (110–11). The fact that she is ten years his senior serves only to 'nourish' his 'passion', since he finds a 'peculiar fascination' in her 'superiority of experience and ripeness of emotion' (115). At their next meeting it is quite clear in what sense he has 'become a man', greeting her with a 'new and maturer light in his eye', kissing her cheek 'almost devotionally' and swearing that her eyes will henceforth be his stars (116–18). Failing to observe their moral resolution not to continue their secret meetings, he proposes to her while the light of their 'little lantern fell upon her beautiful face' without a beam leaking out into the night to betray them (126).

The secrecy of their encounters, of course, the perpetual danger of discovery, increases their erotic excitement, especially in the scene immediately after their wedding when they hide in a small hut to allow the scar caused by her brother's whip to heal. The unspoken delights of their first night as man and wife are brought home by the opening sentence of the following chapter: 'When

Lady Constantine awoke the next morning Swithin was nowhere to be seen' (154), a sentence whose 'erotic charge' has been attributed to the 'romance and adultery' suggested by her continuing under her old name. The narrative thus 'contrives to make marriage seem more shocking, or more romantic, than living in sin' (Bayley, 1982: 62–3).

There is a similar wicked insouciance about the way in which the Bishop of Melchester is made to misread Lady Constantine's sexual satisfaction, her 'recently gratified affection', as 'a sweet serenity, a truly Christian contentment' (*TT*: 178–9; see Sumner, 1982: 79). The treatment of the bishop, who lectures Swithin and loves his wife 'all in one breath' (223) and is fooled into thinking himself the father of their child, caused a certain scandal at the time, a scandal to which Hardy mischievously added by making it quite explicit that the child must have been conceived after the lovers knew their marriage to be invalid. 'There is hardly a single caress in the book outside legal matrimony,' he insisted in the 1895 preface, but there only needed to be one (Taylor, 1982: 134). By making Lady Constantine's husband such a monster and the bishop such a fool Hardy succeeds in enlisting most readers' sympathies with her romance while at the same time investing it with the sweet aura of sin.

Needless to say, Lady Constantine's happiness cannot last. Having allowed Swithin to further his researches abroad and been forced to marry the bishop to make their child legitimate, she has to suffer the young man's return to notice the ravages time has made upon her features:

> The image he had mentally carried out with him to the Cape he had brought home once again as that of the woman he was now to rejoin. But another woman sat before him, and not the original Viviette. (*TT*: 289)

Desire, once more, is portrayed as more a matter of images than of reciprocal relationship. A further bitter twist is added to the story when she dies of sudden joy after he promises nevertheless to marry her. The only figure to be seen as he looks about for help is that of the pretty Tabitha Lark, 'skirting the field with a bounding tread', full of vitality and erotic promise. Hardy later wrote: 'History does not record whether Swithin married Tabitha or not. Perhaps when Lady C. was dead he grew passionately attached to her again, as people often do' (Taylor, 1982: 144). Both possible outcomes are equally ironic, pointing as they do to the uncontrollable nature of desire, the irrationality of the erotic.

All these novels of Hardy's middle period portray desire as something beyond human control, provoked as it is by the lust of the eyes, increased by the attraction of the mysterious and enigmatic, fluctuating and being displaced by chance rather than design. What is interesting about these novels, what distinguishes them from those of his earlier period, is the extent to which women are seen not only as objects of male desire but as subjects, with wishes and desires of their own, who are quite prepared to use the only power they possess, that of attracting men, to their own advantage. The world of the erotic remains beyond all control, however, and their attempts often come to grief, whether on the rock of moral disapproval or on other rocks which the narrative places in their path. Hardy again has it both ways, admiring the spiritedness of their struggles and yet seeming to enjoy the fixes in which they find themselves. Ultimately, of course, the pleasure of the text, the enjoyment for the reader, is voyeuristic. Distanced, uninvolved and removed from all possible danger, he or she can revel in the erotic delights unfolded by the text.

# 5

# A Question of Manliness: Henchard and Fitzpiers

With Hardy's two novels of the late 1880s, *The Mayor of Caster-bridge* and *The Woodlanders*, the focus of attention switches from women to men. Desire remains central in both. *The Mayor of Casterbridge*, for example, has been called 'a nightmare of frustrated desire', Henchard turning from one object to another in a frantic attempt to fill his 'emotional void' (Miller, 1970: 147–8). For Fitzpiers too, the central character in *The Woodlanders*, the object of desire is forever changing, the only constant being his restless search for an outlet for his emotions. Both Henchard and Fitzpiers are contrasted with very different men: the former with Farfrae, more moderate in his desires and self-regulated in his behaviour; the latter with Winterborne, a model of moral rectitude and restraint. These men are all seen through women's eyes, often through the mirrors and windows of their distorted desire. Both novels can be said to question the nature of 'manliness', undermining traditional gender-roles and conventional morality in their exploration of the whole spectrum of human sexuality.

## THE MAYOR OF CASTERBRIDGE

*The Mayor of Casterbridge*, as Hardy recognised in his preface of 1895, 'is more particularly a study of one man's deeds and character' than any other of his novels (*MC*: 33). Henchard, like Heathcliff, is portrayed through geological metaphors, as a man driven by powerful impulses and emotions which belie conscious control, 'the unruly volcanic stuff beneath the rind' of his personality disrupting all attempts at repression. His explosions of rage at Elizabeth-Jane's innocent improprieties are seen as 'the small protruding needle-rocks which suggested rather than revealed what was underneath' (158–9). He is an emotional man, 'the kind of man to whom some human object for pouring out his heat upon – were it emotive or were it choleric – was almost a necessity' (153). The novel traces the transference of this heat from his wife Susan to his mistress Lucetta to his partner Farfrae to the woman he once believed to be his daughter Elizabeth-Jane, the loss of each in turn leaving 'an emotional void in Henchard that he consciously craved to fill' (175). For a time he attempts to live without emotions, abandoning the 'feminine' world of feeling for the 'masculine' world of success. But, to his credit as a human being, he is finally 'unmanned', made to recognise the dominance of his emotions, 'mastered' by the 'weaker' sex.

Henchard is introduced at the beginning of the novel as a classic male chauvinist, preserving a 'perfect silence' as he walks with his wife and daughter, 'reading, or pretending to read, a ballad sheet'. His wife, who keeps 'as close to his side as was possible without actual contact', is clearly used to this treatment: 'far from exhibiting surprise at his ignoring silence she appeared to receive it as a natural thing'. The pair display all the signs of marriage, for no other 'relationship would have accounted for the atmosphere of stale familiarity' which surrounds them. Hardy altered this opening to emphasise still further the distance of the man from his wife in contrast with the closeness of mother and daughter: the only communication is 'an occasional whisper of the woman to the child . . . and the murmured babble of the child in reply' (35–6). Similarly, when the same mother with, as we later learn, a different daughter pass the same way after an interval of nearly twenty years, they walk 'with joined hands . . . the act of simple affection' (51; Showalter, 1979: 104). The female world, unlike the male one, finds room for the expression of feelings.

In selling his wife at Weydon Fair Henchard has been seen to fulfil a deep masculine wish, to act out a common 'male fantasy':

To shake loose from one's wife; to discard that drooping rag of a woman, with her mute complaints and maddening passivity; to escape not by slinking abandonment but through the public sale of her body to a stranger, as horses are sold at the fair; and thus to wrest, through sheer amoral wilfulness, a second chance out of life. (Howe, 1968: 84)

Even Lucetta, the least liberated of women, complains of his selling his wife 'at a fair like a horse or cow' (*MC*: 235). Henchard humiliates his wife, reducing her to an object open to the considered appraisal of potential buyers such as a 'smoking gentleman' who praises her bone structure, which is as good 'as any female in the fair' (41). Later in the novel, when the much-chastened Henchard revisits the fair, he recognises that in abandoning the 'feminine' values of feeling for the 'masculine' values of money, what he 'sacrificed in sentiment was worth as much as what he . . . gained in substance'. By then, of course, even 'his attempts to replace ambition by love had been as fully foiled as his ambition itself' (339).

In the male world of Casterbridge, however, Henchard at first achieves sufficient success to become Mayor. Mother and daughter, peering in through the windows of the King's Arms at the public dinner over which he presides, see an impressive figure, 'a man about forty years of age, of heavy frame, large features, and commanding voice'. His 'flashing black eye' and frightening 'loud laugh', however, suggest to the watching women 'a temperament which would be ready to yield ungrudging admiration to greatness and strength', capable of generous impulses rather than 'a mild and constant kindness' (64). He is respected by the men of Casterbridge for his strength, honesty and perseverance, although another woman discerns 'a bluebeardy look about 'en' (115). He does not in fact murder his wife, but he does see himself as 'something of a woman-hater' (108). 'These cursed women,' he cries when Lucetta refuses to see him on the first evening of her arrival in Casterbridge; 'there's not an inch of straight grain in 'em' (177).

Henchard's dealings with women reveal his roughness in the complicated realm of feeling which he affects to despise. It is not, however, that he lacks emotion but that he is ashamed of it and incapable of giving it expression. He turns away from Elizabeth-Jane, for example, on their first encounter, 'with a wet eye', handing her five guineas which 'tacitly . . . said' to his wife 'that he bought her back again' (98–9). She remains, in other words, an object for which the only means of reparation he can find are financial and material:

Lest she should pine for deeper affection than he could give he made a point of showing some semblance of it in external action. Among other things he had the inner railings, that had smiled sadly in dull rust for the last eighty years, painted a bright green, and the heavy-barred, small-paned Georgian sash windows enlivened with three coats of white. (116)

Like his house, Henchard's emotions are rusty, peering out with difficulty through heavy bars of repression.

Henchard's feelings for Elizabeth-Jane are similarly proprietorial. He tells his wife that he is looking forward to 'seeing my own only child under my roof, as well as my wife' (104) and she does not dare to disabuse him of his belief that Elizabeth-Jane is *his*. In the event, of course, the house is so large and its rooms so 'lofty' that 'the two unassuming women scarcely made a perceptible addition to its contents' (116). While he still thinks her his daughter Henchard comes to feel strongly about her, speaking 'in jerks, and moving like a great tree in a wind' as he reveals his fatherhood to her. 'Don't forget 'twas I gave you your name', he urges with classic patronymic possessiveness, insisting that she change her surname as well (151). Then, on discovering her true parentage and recognising Newson's features in her sleeping countenance, he 'could not endure the sight of her, and hastened away' (154). Deprived of direct family relationship to him she becomes merely a hindrance, undermining his position in the community by failing to lord it over the servants, to speak 'proper' English and to write in 'proper . . . ladies'-hand', the 'bristling characters' which 'were as inseparable a part of refined womanhood as sex itself' (158). Elizabeth-Jane, in consequence, lives in perpetual 'fear of doing anything definable as unlady-like' in her father's eyes (169).

Henchard's conventional views of women are apparent also in his treatment of Lucetta. When a letter arrives from Jersey he finds his own thoughts more interesting than its contents. He delays reading it, dwelling on the envelope as 'a picture, a vision, a vista of past enactments'; reading what Lucetta may have to say becomes simply 'an unimportant finale to conjecture' (145). Lucetta herself, in contrast with the philosophical Elizabeth-Jane, is entirely ladylike, her appearance having all the 'artistic perfection' that fashion can bestow (161). While Elizabeth-Jane labours over Mill, Lucetta finds her mind taxed and her personality defined by her choice of dress. 'Settling upon new clothes is so trying,' she tells Elizabeth-Jane as she contemplates two different gowns spread out upon her bed. '"You are that person" (pointing to one of the arrangements), "or you are *that* totally different person" (pointing to the other), "for the whole of the coming spring".' In the end she decides to become 'the cherry-coloured person', rivalling the attractions of Farfrae's brightly coloured new horse drill as they are both paraded in the market-square. It is typical of her 'feminine' remoteness from the economic base of her society that while Elizabeth-Jane immediately sees that the drill has 'something to do with corn', Lucetta calls it 'a sort of agricultural piano' (192–3).

Henchard, of course, is charmed by Lucetta's ladylike manners, not least the decorousness of her language, which transforms the scandal of their earlier affair, explicitly sexual in the manuscript (374), into mere '*étourderie*' (174). Her 'pleasant manoeuvre' with Elizabeth-Jane, which makes her a pretext for his renewed courtship, causes him to murmur with delight at such typically 'feminine' guile: 'The artful little woman!', although he is less pleased, as we have seen, with the 'airs' she adopts when putting him off (176–7). It is only when she becomes the object of another man's attentions, part of his rivalry with Farfrae, that Henchard's 'smouldering sentiments' are 'fanned into higher and higher inflammation':

> He was discovering that the young woman for whom he once felt a pitying warmth which had been almost chilled out of him by reflection, was, when now qualified with a slight inaccessibility and a more matured beauty, the very being to make him satisfied with life. (200)

His desire for Lucetta becomes a reflection or refraction of his feeling for Farfrae.

It is in the presentation of Henchard's relationship with Farfrae that Hardy goes furthest in undermining conventional notions of 'manliness', for there can be little doubt that the love Henchard bears for the slender and delicate Scot has a sexual component. 'To be sure, to be sure, how that fellow does draw me,' mutters Henchard to himself as he pauses outside Farfrae's hotel to listen to his voice 'through the heart-shaped holes in the window-shutters'. He attempts to rationalise his feeling: 'I suppose 'tis because I'm so lonely' (87). A little later, having persuaded the new-comer to stay in Casterbridge, he disguises his emotion as male camaraderie: 'I am the most distant fellow in the world when I don't care for a man,' he tells Farfrae. 'But when a man takes my fancy he takes it strong' (94).

Elizabeth-Jane notices how quickly the relationship becomes close, needing physical expression:

She saw that Donald and Mr Henchard were inseparables. When walking together Henchard would lay his arm familiarly on his manager's shoulder, as if Farfrae were a younger brother, bearing so heavily that his slight figure bent under the weight.

Henchard's emotions find relief in the occasional 'cannonade of laughter', while Farfrae is simply puzzled by the extent to which he has become 'desirable' in the older man's eyes. There is no doubt, to Elizabeth-Jane's discerning eye, who is the dominant partner in this relationship, her father's 'tigerish affection for the younger man', with his 'slim . . . physical girth', resulting in 'a tendency to domineer' (119–20). She envies the warmth of their relationship, 'the impetuous cordiality' of her father complementing the 'genial modesty' of his manager. 'Friendship between man and man,' she observes with culturally conditioned naivety, 'what a rugged strength there was in it'. Henchard's feelings, however, can turn as easily to hatred as to love and, significantly, the 'seed' that lifts the 'foundation of this friendship', exposing 'a chink in its structure' (126), involves the young Scot being shocked by the ribald punishment Henchard imposes on one of his labourers, making him work without trousers. Outshone by the object of his affections, Henchard dismisses him and even spurns him in public, 'cankered in soul' (144).

It is in wrestling with Farfrae, like Birkin with Gerald Crich in *Women in Love*, that Henchard discovers the depths and complexity of his emotional needs. He lies in wait for the new mayor in the loft of his granaries until, as in so many other erotic scenes in Hardy, the object of his desire is illumined by the light of the setting sun, 'warming' the young man's features 'to a complexion of flame-colour'. The sound of his voice, singing of trust and friendship, warms Henchard still more and even in their desperate clinch 'he gazed upon the lowered eyes of his fair and slim antagonist'. The narrator at this point makes no comment on his inner feelings. But, having brought Farfrae to submission, Henchard himself confesses: 'God is my witness that no man ever loved another as I did thee.' And when Farfrae has gone he is left to contemplate further the unexpected nature and depth of his emotions:

So thoroughly subdued was he that he remained on the sacks in
a crouching attitude, unusual for a man, and for such a man. Its
womanliness sat tragically on the figure of so stern a piece of
virility. (292–7)

Henchard is horribly diminished in his own eyes by discovering
such 'womanly' qualities in himself. He recovers sufficiently to call
out to Farfrae as Lucetta lies in danger, 'my heart is true to you
still' (308). But his love remains unreturned: 'Farfrae had never so
passionately liked Henchard as Henchard had liked him' (349). It
is never an avowedly homosexual relationship, but Henchard's
manliness is clearly more complex than he cares to admit.

'The Unmanning of the Mayor of Casterbridge', of course, the
breaking down of his conventional notions of manliness (Showalter, 1979: 101), is not simply a matter of sexual orientation. It
affects all aspects of his behaviour. He is first described as
'unmanned' when he allows his impulse for revenge over Lucetta
to be softened by pity and sympathy (MC: 274). Even more
significant is the softening of his heart towards Elizabeth-Jane, his
recognition of his need of affection from her. As they worry
together over Lucetta's illness,

> She [Elizabeth-Jane] seemed to him as a pin-point of light. He
> had liked the look of her face as she answered him from the
> stairs. There had been affection in it, and above all things what
> he desired now was affection from anything that was good and
> pure. She was not his own; yet for the first time, he had a faint
> dream that he might get to like her as his own, – if she would
> only continue to love him. (309)

He ceases to domineer over her, even making her breakfast. His lie
to her natural father, seen in the context of this new-found
capacity for love, wins readers' (and eventually Elizabeth-Jane's)
sympathy rather than disapproval, for he has become a different,
altogether more vulnerable, man. The effigy of himself encountered floating down the river after the skimmity-ride can be seen
as 'the symbolic shell of a discarded male self' (Showalter, 1979:
112). In the pervasive animal imagery of the novel he has been
tamed, turned into a 'netted' if not altogether 'fangless lion'
(MC: 324, 330). He becomes so 'morbidly sensitive' that the sound of

wedding bells celebrating Farfrae's final union with Elizabeth-Jane 'quite unmanned him' (343) and he is so 'emolliated' by solitude and sadness when he enters their drawing-room and catches sight of 'the once-despised daughter who had mastered him, and made his heart ache' that he cannot bring himself to talk to her (344–5). He dies, therefore, as he had mostly lived and like his final gift to her, the caged goldfinch, starved of all affection.

Henchard's death at the end of the novel throws a long shadow over Elizabeth-Jane's muted happiness. The much-revised final paragraphs dwell on the harshness of her youthful experience, which also involves an undermining of sexual stereotypes. As she travels with her mother towards Casterbridge early in the novel, the sun shines down upon a face which 'possessed the raw materials of beauty in a promising degree'. Her own ambitions, however, are not limited to the erotic; her 'desire' is 'to see, to hear, and to understand', to 'become a woman of wider know-ledge' (57–8). She falls in love with Farfrae as much on account of his 'serious' attitude to life as his good looks and his impassioned singing (85). As her figure fills out and Farfrae responds to this development in the extraordinary scene in which he blows her clear of chaff, lingering over her hair and neck, her own eyes too contain a 'longing lingering light' as they gaze at his dancing figure (136). But, looking at her reflection in Lacanian self-distrust, she recognises the limits of her sexual attractiveness. Her beauty is 'just enough to make him silly' but 'not enough to keep him so' (140). She is forced to quench her 'incipient interest' in him as 'one-sided, unmaidenly, and unwise', returning to her dusty tomes as the tears 'glide down her peachy cheeks' (160).

Continual experience of disappointment and displacement, of finding that 'what she had desired had not been granted her, and that what had been granted her she had not desired', enables Elizabeth-Jane to learn 'the lesson of renunciation' (204). She even comes to see the comic side of the triangle of desire created by Lucetta, Farfrae and Henchard although she, loving all three, is left out in the cold. Significantly, as Henchard and Farfrae take opposite ends of the same piece of bread and butter, it is torn in two, anticipating the fate of its giver. Guarding herself against such potential disasters by limiting her desires, Elizabeth-Jane also limits her capacity for joy. Life, she feels, in the famous final paragraph of the novel, 'hardly called for effusiveness' while 'happiness was but the occasional episode in a general drama of

pain' (354). It is a sober philosophy based upon sad experience of
the insatiability of desire in a world not designed to satisfy it.


## THE WOODLANDERS

*The Woodlanders* too involves an exploration of 'manliness' in
relation to desire. The philandering Fitzpiers, who positively
cultivates his erotic sensitivity, is contrasted with the 'manly'
Winterborne, whose natural goodness is celebrated by Marty
South in the final words of this novel. Winterborne, like Tess, is
'purely' natural, his moral rectitude and oneness with nature
contrasting with the infidelity and sophistication of his more
cultured rival. Nature and civilisation, in fact, are seen to be
perpetually at odds, with Grace finally rebelling against the
'cultivation' foisted upon her by her indulgent father. The novel,
however, escapes from this simple moralistic mould, which is very
much complicated by the distortions of desire. As the preface to
the much-revised edition of 1896 admits, 'the immortal puzzle –
given the man and woman, how to find a basis for their sexual
relation – is left where it stood.' The novel vouchsafes no answer,
though it clearly questions the institution of marriage. Hardy's
ironic assumption that his readers will have 'no doubt of the
depravity of the erratic heart who feels some second person to be
better suited to his or her tastes than the one with whom he has
contracted to live' (*W*: 33) should not be taken on trust. As in *The
Mayor of Casterbridge*, the only sure defence against the ravages of
desire is found to be renunciation. And that is hardly satisfactory.

    *The Woodlanders* nevertheless begins and ends with Marty South
abrogating desire. As observed by Mr Percomb the hairdresser,
peeping through her firelit window while she shapes her spars,
she forms a pretty enough 'impression-picture', the 'focus of
observation' being her beautiful chestnut hair which the barber
has come to purchase (41). Recognising the hopelessness of her
love for Winterborne she resolves eventually to part with these
locks, laying them on her scrubbed table 'like waving and ropy
weeds over the washed white bed of a stream' and resolutely
refusing to notice her 'deflowered visage' in a mirror (51).
Illumined later by the light of the moon as she lies by her father's
coffin, she is found to possess, like Elizabeth-Jane, 'the repose of a
guileless soul that had nothing more left on earth to lose, except a

life which she did not over-value' (137). Love for her is encapsu-
lated in the sight of two large birds 'tumbling one over the other
into the hot ashes at their feet' before flying apart 'with a singed
smell' to be 'seen no more' (173). Again like Elizabeth-Jane, she
learns through constant disappointment the lesson of renunciation, 'always doomed to sacrifice desire to obligation' (178). She is
last seen at the end of the novel, again lit by the chaste rays of the
moon, stooping over Winterborne's grave, 'the contours of
womankind so undeveloped as to be scarcely perceptible . . . a
being who had rejected with indifference the attribute of sex for
the loftier quality of abstract humanism' (393).

Winterborne himself has his life ruined and finally ended by
desire. The way it plays havoc with his judgement is at first comic,
as when, obsessed with the way in which the snowflakes settle on
the curls of Grace Melbury's hair, he finds himself outbidding his
father for his favourite lots of timber. He suffers agonies of
embarrassment over such disasters as the slug she finds on her
plate, well-boiled though his man warrants it. He is forever
symbolically poking the embers of his hearth as he talks about
Grace, who grows to appreciate his 'undiluted manliness' only
after she is irrevocably united with the unworthy Fitzpiers (236).
Her fascination with her husband having evaporated, the two
lovers are trapped by the laws of matrimony, which appear all the
more arbitrary after her hopes are raised by talk of new possibilities of divorce.

Throughout the tantalising period when it appears that their
love may be made legal, Winterborne does his best to restrain his
feelings. On meeting her in the woods, for example, his eyes
'suppressedly looked his pleasure' (306). On one occasion only
does he rebel against repression and that is when Grace, believing
her father to have found a new hope of divorce, deliberately
encourages him to kiss her:

> Winterborne, though fighting valiantly against himself all this
> while – though he would have protected Grace's good repute as
> the apple of his eye, was a man; and as Desdemona said, men are
> not gods. In the face of the agonizing seductiveness shown by
> her, in her unenlightened school-girl simplicity about the laws
> and ordinances, he betrayed a man's weakness. Since it was so –
> since it had come to this, that Grace, deeming herself free to do it,
> was virtually asking him to demonstrate that he loved her – since

he could demonstrate it only too truly – since life was short and love was strong – he gave way to the temptation . . . simply accepting the present and what it brought, deciding once in his life to clasp in his arms her he had watched over and loved so long. (318–19)

This embrace, 'prolonged' though it is 'an unconscionable time' (319), represents his only fall from propriety.

In the end, of course, Winterborne gives up his life rather than stain Grace's honour. Relinquishing the shelter of his hut to her, he exacerbates his illness, ignoring even her direct pleas, added by Hardy in the 1896 edition: 'I want you here!' and 'Come to me, my dearest! I don't mind what they say or what they think of us any more' (336–7; Kramer, 1981: 287). The narrator makes much of 'the purity of his nature, his freedom from the grosser passions, his scrupulous delicacy' in doing so, all of which are finally recognised by the frantic object of his love as she kisses his dying hands, face and hair (341). But implicit in her recognition that the animals who cluster round his quarters 'knew neither law nor sin' (333) is the suggestion that Winterborne might have done better to obey nature in this respect as well. Grace herself is certainly punished rather than rewarded by the preservation of her marriage. As Hardy wrote with regard to a projected dramatisation of the novel, 'the ending of the story – hinted rather than stated – is that the heroine is doomed to an unhappy life with an inconstant husband' (*Life*: 230). For, as Melbury is made to say in the 1896 edition, 'the woman walks and laughs somewhere at this very moment whose neck he'll be cooling next year as he does hers tonight' (*W*: 389; Kramer, 1981: 335).

The man in question, Edred Fitzpiers, is very much the centre of the novel Hardy first offered to Macmillan with the potential alternative title 'Fitzpiers at Hintock' (Kramer, 1981: 7). He is the complete opposite of Winterborne; far from restraining his sexual impulses he deliberately indulges them, building an elaborate erotic superstructure on the natural base of desire. He has no illusions about love. Having treated Winterborne to a recital of Shelley at his most ethereal on 'the bright shade of some immortal dream', he proceeds to analyse the dynamics of desire with all the philosophical sophistication of a Parisian post-structuralist:

Human love is a subjective thing . . . it is joy accompanied by an idea that we project against any suitable object in the line of our vision, just as the rainbow iris is projected against an oak, ash or elm tree indifferently. So that if any other young lady had appeared instead of the one who did appear, I should have felt just the same interest in her, and have quoted precisely the same lines from Shelley about her, as about this one I saw. (*W*: 168)

All this is clearly beyond Winterborne, who insists that what Fitzpiers feels 'is what we call being in love down in these parts'. If he *is* in love, Fitzpiers counters, then it is with 'something in my own head, and no thing-in-itself outside it' (147).

Fitzpiers, then, prefers 'the ideal world to the real', not even bothering to pursue Grace when he sees her dealing elegantly with the painted gate observable from his window, indulging instead in a 'conjectural pursuit'. His erotic dreams, stimulated by leisure and poetry, immediately focus upon her. While a lonely 'old man dreams of an ideal friend', according to the narrator, a young man in the same circumstances will

think rather of an ideal mistress, and at length the rustle of a woman's dress, the sound of her voice, or the transit of her form across the field of his vision, will enkindle his soul with a flame that blinds his eyes. (154)

Fitzpiers, in fact, can hardly believe his eyes when the form that fills his inner visions appears reflected in his living-room mirror. Grace sees those eyes open, 'gazing wonderingly at her', while he wakes to an awareness 'that the lovely form which seemed to have visited him in a dream was no less than the real presentation' of the timber merchant's daughter (158). Brought into close contact with her in his narrow porch, where she excites him by brushing his coat with her elbow, 'he awoke from looking at her as at a piece of live statuary' – another Lacanian symbol of the artificiality of desire, its capacity to create objects in its own image, to celebrate his discovery of an object which does indeed mirror his dreams.

Fitzpiers's infatuation with Grace is nurtured by precisely the right conditions, fed by 'cursory encounters' which build 'acquaintance' rather than knowledge. He abandons his original 'lax notion' of a 'vulgar intimacy' with her, both the 'laxity' and the 'intimacy' being 1896 additions to clarify his sexual freedom (165; Kramer, 1981: 128–9), and is carried forward into full-blooded courtship 'on the wave of his desire' (184). He makes no attempt to disguise 'his irreverent views of marriage' (196), which fails to change his philandering nature. Sickened by his infidelity with Suke Damson and Mrs Charmond, Grace feels that he must have married her for money. But the narrator corrects her:

> the love of men like Fitzpiers is unquestionably of such quality as to bear division and transference. He had indeed once declared, though not to her, that on one occasion he had noticed himself to be possessed by five distinct infatuations at the same time. (239)

The number, of course, is immaterial; what matters is the insatiability of sexual desire.

The sexual appetite of 'men like Fitzpiers' is made increasingly more explicit in later versions of the story. His seduction of Suke Damson, for example, does not seem to have been part of Hardy's first intentions. In a deleted passage in the manuscript, they implausibly bed down for the night in separate haycocks (Kramer, 1981: 27, 399). In the serial version they restrict themselves to a single kiss; in the first edition Fitzpiers 'kissed her again'; while from 1896 he 'pressed her close to him', remaining silent 'on the hay'. Serial readers were also deprived of the highly erotic, totally implicit, final line of the chapter: 'It was daybreak before Fitzpiers and Suke Damson re-entered Little Hintock' (W: 180; Kramer, 1981: 44, 142).

That Fitzpiers does not restrict his re-entering of Suke Damson to Midsummer Night is made clear by another addition of 1896 which refers to 'the intimacy *established* in the hayfield' but evidently continued beyond it (200: Kramer, 1981: 44, 161; emphasis added). This, of course, is confirmed by Grace catching sight of 'a female figure, wrapped in a large cloak' emerging in the early hours of the morning from Fitzpiers's front door. The 1896 edition adds to the sexual suggestiveness of this scene with an explicit reference to her 'night-dress' (196; Kramer, 1981: 158). Hardy's battles over *Tess* and *Jude*, it has been suggested, along with his own marriage difficulties, had made him 'combative and defiant' at the time of these revisions. It is in the 1896 edition too that Grace's immortal response to Mrs Charmond first appears: 'O my great God. . . . He's had you!' (272; Kramer, 1981: 44–5, 227–8). Also in this edition, when all three women cluster round Fitzpiers's bed after his accident (having been restricted in the serial to the hallway), Grace is given her cutting remark: 'Wives all, let's enter together' (288; Kramer, 1981: 45, 242).

The erotic quality of the depiction of Fitzpiers's relation with Mrs Charmond, however, as in Hardy's earlier work, relies on indirectness, leaving as much as possible to the imagination. The mysterious owner of Hintock House, who appears 'ripely handsome' even to Marty South (71), is the subject of much speculation among male woodlanders. Creedle, for example, reports his brother-in-law's view that she must be a 'wicked woman' to wear dresses cut as low as hers (57). She herself talks archly of 'man-traps' even to Grace, revealing 'that oblique-mannered softness' common in 'women who lingeringly smile their meanings rather than speak them, who inveigle rather than prompt' (89–90). The seductive picture she presents to Fitzpiers when she summons him so unnecessarily to attend her is described in vivid detail:

He was shown into a room at the top of the staircase, cosily and femininely draped, where by the light of the shaded lamp he saw a woman of elegant figure reclining upon a couch in such a position as not to disturb a pile of magnificent hair on the crown of her head. A deep purple dressing-gown formed an admirable foil to the peculiarly rich brown of her hair-plaits; her left arm, which was naked nearly up to the shoulder, was thrown upwards, and between the fingers of her right hand she held a cigarette, while she idly breathed from her delicately curled lips a thin stream of smoke towards the ceiling. (216–17)

Everything in her house, from the furnishings to the purchased hair, is carefully designed to add the erotic charms of culture to her fading gifts of nature. She keeps red-shaded lamps and candles burning throughout the day to create a 'rosy passionate lamplight' in which the erotic imagination can flourish. The artificiality of the whole relationship is reinforced by the image of painting in which the former lovers are seen to make their previous encounter in the romantic alps 'a canvas for infinite fancies, idle dreams, luxurious melancholies, and pretty, adoring assertions' (223).

Perhaps the most suggestive scene involving Fitzpiers and Mrs Charmond is that in which he is observed by his father-in-law removing her glove in the woods:

Fitzpiers clasped her hanging hand, and, while she still remained in the same listless attitude, looking volumes into his eyes, he stealthily unbuttoned her glove, and stripped her hand of it by rolling back the gauntlet over the fingers, so that it came off inside out. He then raised her hand to his mouth, she still reclining passively, watching him as she might have watched a fly upon her dress. (247)

Mrs Charmond, however, suffers for her arrogance, finding herself against her will genuinely in love with her married neighbour, failing to persuade either herself or Grace that she is merely trifling with him. She is 'seized by a hand of velvet', becoming 'a passion incarnate' (262), her violent passion leading to a violent end.

The final irony of the novel, the most absurd of Fitzpiers's many infatuations, is his falling in love for a second time with his wife. The simple woodland mind, exemplified by Tim Tangs, cannot understand 'the fineness of tissue which could take a deep, emotional – almost also an artistic – pleasure in being the yearning *innamorato* of a woman he once had deserted' (374). Even more incomprehensible to anyone ignorant of the distortions of desire is that her proclaimed infidelity with Giles is the stimulus for his renewed interest: 'the man whom Grace's matrimonial fidelity could not keep faithful was stung into passionate throbs of interest concerning her by her avowal of the contrary' (359). Forever 'a subtlist in emotions', he prolongs the pleasure of suspense by delaying any practical proposals which would 'put an end to these exotics' (363). He positively revels in the foreplay of courtship: the 'very restraint that he was obliged to exercise . . . fed his flame' (381). His slow build-up to reunion is hastened to its climax, however, by the sight of his beloved wife stripped to the waist by the jaws of a man-trap. Once securely possessed, as her long-suffering father appreciates, Grace can look forward to a future of infidelity and neglect.

Grace herself, then, suffers disgracefully at the hands of both her husband and her creator. Hardy is reported to have disliked her:

He said that Grace never interested him much; he was provoked with her all along. If she would have done a really self-abandoned, impassioned thing (gone off with Giles), he could have made a fine tragic ending to the book, but she was too commonplace and straitlaced, and he could not make her. (Boumelha, 1982: 105)

He did, however, in the 1896 edition, give her those heartfelt pleas for Giles to ignore propriety and come to her, and the fact that both her husband and her father at first believe her to be guilty of the adultery she confesses, from a mixture of anger and regret, has been seen as at least a recognition of 'the possibilities of her sexual drive' (Kramer, 1981: 46). But she never really escapes from her early characterisation by her neighbours as 'a teuny, delicate piece . . . as nesh as her mother was' (*W*: 58), the spoilt apple of her father's eye.

Hardy's difficulties with Grace are openly confessed on her first appearance in the novel, delicately holding herself back from Winterborne's generous affection:

> It would have been difficult to describe Grace Melbury with precision, either then or at any time. Nay, from the highest point of view, to precisely describe a human being, the focus of a universe, how impossible! But apart from transcendentalism, there never probably lived a person who was in herself more completely a *reductio ad absurdum* of attempts to appraise a woman, even externally, by items of face and figure.

What people see, the narrator insists, is merely her external image, decked in the latest fashion, 'something that was not she . . . a shape in the gloom' (69). Like other obscure objects of desire she is frequently seen lit up, for instance by the fire in her parlour which 'irradiated' her face in Winterborne's eyes (76). On another occasion he sees her lighting several candles in order to estimate her own attractions in the mirror. Fitzpiers too sees her features irradiated by the light of the moon on Midsummer Night.

The greatest difficulty with Grace, however, is in the depiction of her own desire, which seems decidedly lukewarm. She is interested in Fitzpiers before they meet, the information about him gleaned from Grammer Oliver feeding 'kaleidoscopic dreams' combining him with Giles (82). She is particularly susceptible to his presence, feeling an uneasiness which takes her breath away. Her love for him, however, is 'based upon mystery and strangeness', evaporating with 'the intimacy of common life' (233). Her father may suggest, in another addition of 1896, that she takes him back simply out of sexual desire: 'Let

her take him back to her bed if she will' (389; Kramer, 1981: 335).
But this is by no means clear.

Grace's love for Winterborne, too, is often lukewarm and
ambivalent, rarely escaping from a distaste for his roughness and
lack of cultivation. In a manner the narrator calls 'peculiar to
women's nature' she treats him with a mixture of distance and
affection, 'entertaining a tender pity for the object of her own
unnecessary coldness' (114). She blows hottest towards him
immediately after rejecting him, changing Marty South's lines
about him losing his Grace along with his houses out of an
impulse of sympathy he failed to enjoy as 'her promised lover'
(140). Even when she is drawn towards his 'undiluted manliness',
when he looks and smells 'like Autumn's very brother', when 'her
passionate desire for primitive life' can be seen in her face,
encouraging him to caress the flower in her bosom, she suddenly
draws back, reprimanding him with frosty propriety: 'What are
you doing, Giles Winterborne?' (235-7). It is not that she lacks
desire. Later, in his absence, 'her fancy wove about him a more
romantic tissue than it could have done if he had stood before her
with all the specks and flaws inseparable from concrete humanity'
(305). But she lacks the courage of her dreams. In a final failure of
nerve, a final triumph of repressive culture over nature, she allows
him to sacrifice his life for her name. Hardy's revisions of 1896,
reducing the size of Giles's hut from two rooms to one and making
her cry out for him to join her, fail to rescue her from the implicit
charge of frigidity. Her punishment, as we have seen, is to know
the difference between the two men, to see 'how little
acquirements and culture weigh beside sterling personal character', and to be saddled for life with the wrong one.

Far from reinforcing the conventional morality of restraint, then,
*The Woodlanders* questions both the morality and the effectiveness
of social institutions such as marriage in the face of natural sexual
impulses. In terms of conventional morality, of course,
Winterborne is the hero and Fitzpiers the villain of the piece. The
narrator himself, as we have seen, sometimes encourages such
casting. Yet such is the nature of sexual desire, in 'men like
Fitzpiers' at least, that conventional morality remains powerless
against it while even men like Winterborne gain little from their
restraint. The novel, in other words, is deeply split between
admiration of the 'manliness' of Winterborne's ideal and recognition of its unreality.

# 6

# Diabolical Dames and
# Grotesque Desires:
# The Short Stories

Hardy published nearly fifty short stories in a variety of periodicals from 1865 to 1900, collecting the majority of them for republication in four volumes: *Wessex Tales*, a set of rural romances drawn from the folklore of the West Country; *A Group of Noble Dames*, recounting the perverse desires of a number of aristocratic ladies of the seventeenth and eighteenth centuries; *Life's Little Ironies*, a macabre series of illustrations of the tricks fate plays upon loving men and women; and *A Changed Man*, a miscellaneous collection of tales whose central theme is the chaos introduced into human lives by the irresistible dictates of desire. Each of these volumes contributes to Hardy's exploration of the erotic. Like the short stories of Hawthorne and Poe, of which so much has been made by post-structuralist and psychoanalytic critics, they lead beyond the 'normal' characterisation of the realistic novel to consider those areas of the psyche which are abnormal, obsessive and irrational.

Hardy's short stories are often dismissed as melodramatic and clumsy because they are full of such abnormal characters and perverse situations. Even when they have been recognised as instances of his 'interest in psychology, especially in its bizarre and unusual aspects', they have been criticised for their fixation upon single oddities of character at the expense of the 'whole personality' (Sumner, 1981: 18). Yet Hardy can be seen to be challenging the liberal humanist notion of coherent personality, deliberately focusing on the incoherence of human behaviour, in particular the irrationality of desire. The short stories demonstrate a particular interest in the 'uncanny' in Freud's famous definition, 'that class of the frightening which leads back to what is known of

89

old and long familiar', combining the 'strange' with the 'common-place', breaking down that 'distinction between imagination and reality' upon which sanity is based and shedding doubt on the stable certainties of the rational world (Keys, 1985: 111). The *Wessex Tales* in particular draw on familiar traditions of folklore to undermine any belief in the simplicity of country life (Brady, 1982: 48–9).

## WESSEX TALES

At least five of the seven stories written between 1879 and 1888 which were collected as *Wessex Tales* focus on the dreams and illusions of desire. 'The Melancholy Hussar of the German Legion' tells a familiar tale of infatuation with the exotic and unknown, a local girl finding herself fascinated by the melancholy face of a young German soldier. The language barrier between them speeds the process of her infatuation, for 'the eyes . . . helped out the tongue and . . . the lips helped out the eyes' (*WT*: 50). Refusing to see him in the same serious light as someone who spoke the same language,

> She no longer checked her fancy for the Hussar. . . . The young foreign soldier was almost an ideal being to her, with none of the appurtenances of an ordinary house-dweller; one who had descended she knew not whence, and would disappear she knew not whither; the subject of a fascinating dream – no more. (53)

She is quite shocked when he proposes, for such a 'practical step had not been in her mind in relation to such an unrealistic person as he was' (54). The Hussar is captured and shot for desertion, leaving her to contemplate her unfaithful fiancé's departing gift, 'a very handsome looking-glass in a frame of *repoussé* silverwork' (59). Her self-reflexive desire, it is implied, will no doubt find new objects on which to reshape itself.

'The Withered Arm' is the most bizarre of the *Wessex Tales*, concerned as it is with the magical powers of a jealous woman. It has been called 'an essay in the pathology of sexual jealousy, . . . a psychological fable' exploring that uncanny area of strange coincidence determined by the forces beyond our conscious control

(Keys, 1985: 106). It begins with a neglected woman sending her son to report on his father's new bride. The lad's 'hard gaze' takes in every ounce of her charm, 'every feature, shade, and contour distinct, from the curve of her little nostril, to the colour of her eyes', lit up by the evening sun. He notices not only how 'nice and red' her mouth is but how her gown 'whewed and whistled' against the pews in church (*WT*: 68–70), culture combining with nature to give a clear indication of her erotic attraction even to the boy.

On the basis of her son's evidence and that of the village gossip, the neglected Rhoda is able to build up 'a mental image' of her rival, as 'realistic as a photograph' and sufficient for a vivid dream in which

> the young wife, in the pale silk dress and white bonnet, but with features shockingly distorted, and wrinkled by age, was sitting upon her chest as she lay . . . the blue eyes peered cruelly into her face, and then the figure thrust forward its left hand mockingly, so as to make the wedding-ring it wore glitter in Rhoda's eyes. (71)

The dream vision is clearly a reflection of Rhoda's jealousy and its deformity a product of her wish-fulfilment. Her vindictive desires are fulfilled in the following sequence of the dream, in which she seizes the bride's mocking left arm and whirls the spectre on to the floor.

But it is not only in the dream that Rhoda achieves her revenge. On waking in a cold sweat she continues to feel the arm within her grasp while the bride actually suffers the resultant injuries, which grow progressively worse until the conjuror to whom she turns as a last resort recommends the touch of a corpse as the only remedy. The corpse she chooses, however, in another uncanny coincidence, turns out to be Rhoda's son, unjustly condemned to hang for arson. Rhoda catches hold of her bare arm, as in the dream, and causes her instant death. The story baffles its readers, breaking down all certainty about what is real and unreal, conscious and unconscious.

Everything is beyond the control of the unfortunate Mr Barnet, one of the two 'Fellow-Townsmen', who never manages to attain the object of his desire, which remains fixed on his first love, Lucy Saville. He comforts himself during his unhappy marriage to a dominating and wilful woman by meditating on the beauties of

Lucy's face, reminding himself of 'the Raffaelesque oval of its contour' by paying her a visit (103) and projecting a 'gaze' of longing on to the curl of smoke which rises from her chimney 'as from a fire new kindled' (117) at the very moment that his wife's body lies believed drowned upon his bed. His wife, however, recovers as a result of his dutiful attentions and proceeds to live just long enough for Lucy to marry the bereaved Mr Downe and thus remain inaccessible to Mr Barnet, who returns after an interval of twenty-one years to find her once more free to marry. She at first refuses him, changing her mind too late to prevent his disappearing for ever unsatisfied. The irony is that Mr Downe is blessed with two marvellous wives whom he takes almost for granted. Possession once more reduces desire, which survives in his fellow-townsman only through perpetual frustration.

Marriage and desire are portrayed throughout the *Wessex Tales* as mutually incompatible. Farmer Charles Darton, for instance, who congratulates himself at the beginning of 'Interlopers at the Knap' on his resolve to do the sensible thing and marry the good-hearted Sally in place of the superior Helena, the first object of his affections, soon finds his old desire reawakened when he encounters Helena in Sally's house wearing the dress he had bought for Sally to marry in. Sally discovers them with their eyes 'fixed' upon each other, the farmer unable to stop 'looking at Helena's dress and outline, and listening to her voice like a man in a dream' (163–5). None of the three participants in this scene knows, at this stage, how the other two relate to each other. It transpires that Helena has married Sally's brother, who has returned from Australia to die. This, of course, leaves Helena free to marry the farmer, only for him to find the reality of marriage an inevitable disappointment, a pale reflection of the delights of desire.

The last of the *Wessex Tales*, 'The Distracted Preacher', plays with the struggle in the mind of a Wesleyan minister between the delights of the erotic and the demands of his conscience. This 'lovable youth, who won upon his female hearers as soon as they saw and heard him' (183), is delighted to find that his widowed landlady, whose first entrance is announced by a provocative 'rustle of garments', is

> a fine and extremely well-made young woman, with dark hair, a
> wide, sensible, beautiful forehead, eyes that warmed him before

he knew it, and a mouth that was in itself a picture to all appreciative souls. (185)

He does not see much of his 'enkindling landlady' since she limits her availability in the deliberate hope of increasing his interest. But the fact that she refers in a slip of the tongue to her 'first husband' makes it clear even to the minister that she 'had thought pretty frequently of a second' (191). He spends a 'titillating fortnight' being allowed only the occasional glimpse of her 'seductive eyes'. Too often, for his taste, there is 'no Lizzy Newberry and no sweet temptations' (192–4). Excited by the mystery of her night-time absences and an independence of manner which 'would have kept from flagging the passion of a far more mutable man' (203), he eventually discovers that she is involved in smuggling.

The combination of drink, sex and smuggling proves irresistible. It is symbolised in a scene in which the young widow offers to cure the minister's cold by uncovering a secret supply of liquor under the singing-gallery of the church, and they refill the keg with water which he sucks from her 'pretty lips' by means of the pressure produced by alternately squeezing and releasing the keg. He even accompanies her on a mission during which their cheeks come into accidental contact as they peer out at the Customs men from their concealed position. His conscience finally forces him to demand that she cease her smuggling if she is to become his wife. The reader is given alternative endings: that of the magazine, in which she gives up smuggling in order to become a dutiful minister's wife and that, according to a footnote added to the collected version, which 'would have been preferred by the writer', in which she sticks to her smuggling. The latter ending certainly captures the spirit in which the whole story is told, the mischievous delight in the sweetness of sin and the impossibility of reconciling the dutiful and the erotic.

None of these macabre stories is 'realistic' at the level of plot or characterisation. They are not long enough to prepare readers for the melodramatic twists with which they are filled. But in terms of the vagaries of desire, the absence of what conventional criticism would call 'convincing' and 'coherent' characterisation becomes a virtue. Acting upon impulse in response to uncontrollable drives, the protagonists of these tales perform the most extraordinary antics, all of which serve to demonstrate the absurdity and unpredictability of human emotions. Hardy abandons realism for a more complex 'reality' beyond the reach of conscious control.

## A GROUP OF NOBLE DAMES

Hardy himself described *A Group of Noble Dames* as 'rather a frivolous piece of work' written 'in a sort of desperation during a fit of low spirits' (*CL* I: 239). The stories are supposedly narrated by the ancient male members of the Wessex Antiquarian Club, who seem to regard the subjects of their stories as of little more interest than the stuffed birds, deformed butterflies and prehistoric dung-mixens which form their surroundings. They interrupt from time to time to comment on the subtlety of their 'psychological studies' and on 'the dreamy and impulsive nature of woman' (*GND*: 131). But they are clearly unreliable as narrators, providing an ironic reflection of the main themes of the collection, the irrationality of desire and the conflict between passion and convention. The noble dames themselves, so much more vital than the antiquarian members, can be seen as victims of social rules, in particular of marriage. They retain a certain fascination, distanced as they are both by time and by class from most of their lovers and most of their readers (Brady, 1982: 51–3, 93). They also illustrate many of the erotic features noticed in Hardy's earlier work, in particular the perversity of desire, its construction of illusory images which are all too easily displaced.

'Barbara of the House of Grebe' is perhaps the best-known of these stories, partly because of the attack launched upon it by T.S. Eliot, who saw it as a vivid illustration of the entry of the diabolic into modern literature (Eliot, 1934: 58). Its heroine, like the archaeologist in Thomas Mann's much-analysed *Gradiva*, falls in love with a statue, that Lacanian symbol of objectified desire. She begins the tale 'a good and pretty girl' but then elopes with the impoverished Edmond Willowes, who has little to recommend him apart from his looks. Sir John and Lady Grebe accept the married couple only on condition that the husband undertake a continental tour to remedy some of the defects of his education and it is on this trip, heroically rescuing others from a fire in Venice, that he becomes so badly disfigured that his wife cannot repress the horror she feels on seeing him, reproach herself though she does for being a 'slave to mere eyesight' (*GND*: 63).

The unwanted husband disappears and dies, only for a statue commissioned on his tour to be sent on to the now remarried Barbara. She falls hopelessly in love all over again, forgetting the 'mutilated features' of the real man in favour of the perfect beauty of his image. 'What are you doing?' demands her second husband, Lord Uplandtowers, discovering her 'lost in reverie' before the statue. 'I am looking at my husb— my statue,' she stammers in parapractic reply (67), for this is the image she married. Enshrining the statue in a secret recess of her boudoir, she steals there in the middle of the night and is seen by her husband

> standing with her arms clasped tightly round the neck of Edmond, and her mouth on his. The shawl which she had thrown round her night-clothes had slipped from her shoulders, and her long white robe and pale face lent her the blanched appearance of a second statue embracing the first. (69)

Two images intertwine in utterly 'unreal' relationship testifying only to the wife's 'intensity of feeling'. The outraged lord, anticipating the horrors of aversion therapy (Sumner, 1980: 230–1), employs a local artist to disfigure the statue in precisely the same manner as the original, destroying her fantasy but also, as a final irony, reducing her to a clinging dependant without the 'resource' that the 'mental world of her own' had provided (*GND*: 75). Human nature, it is implied, relies upon fantasy and illusion for survival.

Three of the other stories in this collection, while illustrating the perversity of desire, end in apparently happy marriages. 'The First Countess of Wessex' is initially so eager to escape the embraces of her older husband that she deliberately contracts smallpox before making a dramatic exit through an upstairs window in order to join her handsome young lover. When he rejects her, repelled by her disfigured face, she returns to her husband, whose patience and forbearance she learns to appreciate. 'The Honourable Laura' reaches a similarly happy conclusion when the husband whom her Italian operatic lover attempted to murder and whom she nursed penitently back to health returns after an absence of twelve years to renew their relationship. 'Anna, Lady Baxby', having resolved to leave her Royalist husband for her Parliamentary brother, changes her mind when she is mistaken for her husband, escaping at night in his hat and cloak, by a local wench waiting for a secret assignation. Seeing him as an object of another's desire ironically rekindles her own erotic interest in him.

Most of the marriages depicted in these stories, however, as one might expect, fail to satisfy the demands of these diabolical dames. 'The Marchioness of Stonehenge' 'perversely and passionately' fixes her affections upon an unremarkable poor man, 'stimulated' by seeing him as the object of another's desire but losing interest once they are married. The plain 'Lady Mottisfont' has her illusory marital bliss destroyed by an exotic Italian contessa while the marriages of 'Lady Icenway' and 'Squire Petrick's Lady' bear equally disastrous fruit, the former remaining barren in spite of employing her first husband as a gardener to make good the incapacity of her second, the latter managing to convince herself that her legitimate son is really the product of an earlier illicit liaison, which turns out to have been 'a delicate ideal dream' (129), a product of her imagination. 'Lady Penelope' actually fulfils her mocking promise to marry all three of her suitors in turn, thereby coming under suspicion for murder, while 'The Duchess of Hamptonshire', a girl of 'extraordinary beauty' (149), becomes enamoured of a local curate with whom she has a 'sweet and secret understanding' (151). She escapes from the duke she is forced to marry, hiding on board the ship on which her lover is emigrating, only to die of fever during the voyage and to be buried at sea, anonymously, in a service conducted by the curate himself, who returns to England, having spent ten years 'dreaming of her', finally to discover the dreadful truth.

Desire, in these stories at least, can only be fulfilled in dreams and illusions. The real world offers at best a contentment attainable only after the death of desire. None of these stories, of course, should be taken very seriously: they represent the mild diversions of a group of cynical old men. But they illustrate, with grim and sometimes grotesque humour, the illusions of reciprocal relationship. None of these noble ladies falls in love with a 'real' object but with a series of objectifications of her desire. The attempt to regulate or control such desire, however, as in the case of the unfortunate curate, meets with little success. There is no moral to be drawn. The whole subject becomes merely a matter for sardonic observation.

## LIFE'S LITTLE IRONIES

The illusion of reciprocal relationship is very much at the centre of

*Life's Little Ironies*, a series of stories first published between 1882 and 1893 which focus once more on the fascinating but false visions produced by the erotic imagination, the gap between the actual object of desire and the image the lover sees. Hardy's irony in these tales has been seen to combine the tragic and the farcical (Brady, 1982: 156). The results of their illusions, from the viewpoint of the protagonists, tend to be tragic while the attempts made by society to control desire through marriage can only appear absurd to the eyes of a dispassionate observer.

'A Few Crusted Characters', the last story in the book, employs the device of multiple narration as various travellers in a carrier's van bring a returning exile from their village up to date on the comic cycle of courtship and marriage that has taken place in his absence. Two cousins, for example, having become engaged to girls unexcitingly similar to themselves, swap partners on the eve of their wedding with disastrous results. A philanderer ends up playing off three prospective fiancées in the same wagon. Similar tales of illusory and unrequited passion reinforce the notion that desire eludes all attempts at its regulation.

A well-meaning attempt to put right the wrong done to a woman twenty years earlier is the subject of 'For Conscience' Sake', in which a guilt-ridden bachelor discovers the woman he abandoned passing herself off as a widowed dancing instructor. She is hardly the same person but he persists in his penitential proposal, accidentally putting at risk his daughter's prospect of marriage to a respectable curate who starts to suspect the older couple's 'new' relationship. The bachelor is forced to abandon his mistress for a second time, acknowledging that 'whatever the remedy may be in such a case it is not marriage' (*LLI*: 57). In 'A Tragedy of Two Ambitions', two self-righteous sons make an even more dramatic sacrifice of their consciences, allowing their embarrassing drunken father to drown within earshot rather than ruin the marriage prospects of their sister, a 'sylph-like' creature who captivates a wealthy and lecherous local landowner (69–70). Marriage is also seen as a vehicle for upward social mobility by a priggish young clergyman in 'The Son's Veto', who stands firmly in the way of his mother's remarriage to the gardener she had first loved, preferring to see her pine away and die rather than satisfy such base desires.

The irrational, uncontrollable nature of sexual attraction is conveyed through the metaphor of music in 'The Fiddler of the

Reels'. Car'line, 'a pretty, invocating, weak-mouthed girl', finds herself 'unable to shake off the strange infatuation' she has for Wat Ollamor, a 'woman's man . . . envied for his power over unsophisticated maidenhood' and nicknamed 'Mop' for his abundance of hair (126–9). Even after her marriage to the worthy Ned Hipcroft she cannot resist the sound of Mop's fiddle, dancing fanatically to his music and suffering 'excruciating spasms, a sort of blissful torture' (140–1), which overthrows every conscious concern – even for the welfare of her daughter, whom Mop abducts.

The two stories in this collection which most clearly reveal the illusory nature of desire are those which Hardy took great care in revising. 'An Imaginative Woman' tells the story of an 'impressionable, palpitating creature' whose husband's 'obtuseness' causes her to let off 'her delicate and ethereal emotions in imaginative occupations, day-dreams, and night-sighs' (1–2). The ill-assorted couple happen, by chance, to rent the seaside rooms of one of her favourite poets, Robert Trewe. Having exposed both her vanity and her Lacanian self-doubt by 'testing the reflecting powers of the mirror in the wardrobe door' (4), she settles down to reread his poems and to luxuriate in his 'circumambient' presence in the room. She even tries on his clothes, and when she hears that there is a photograph of him concealed in a frame in the room she can hardly contain her excitement. She puts off the moment of Trewthe, however, the longer to enjoy the erotic delights of delay:

> After her light dinner Ella idled about the shore with the children till dusk, thinking of the yet uncovered photograph in her room with a serene sense of something ecstatic to come. For, with the subtle luxuriance of fancy in which this young woman was an adept, on learning that her husband was to be absent that night she had refrained from incontinently rushing upstairs and opening the picture-frame, preferring to reserve the inspection till she could be alone, and a more romantic tinge be imparted to the occasion by silence, candles, solemn sea and stars outside, than was afforded by the garish afternoon sunlight. (11–12)

Everything, in other words, is carefully prepared for a positive orgy of eroticism. As the story develops we learn to read the words 'romantic' and 'imaginative' as synonyms for illusory and unreal. Eventually Ella goes to bed, where she makes more elaborate 'preparations' for the final gratification of her 'passionate curiosity . . . first getting rid of superfluous garments', erotic defamiliarisation for undressing, before indulging in 'several pages of Trewe's tenderest utterances'. At last she takes out the photograph, which reveals 'a luxuriant black moustache' and 'large dark eyes' and to which she murmurs in her 'lowest, richest, tenderest tones', gazing at it so long that she falls into a reverie before finally kissing it. Such is the swoon into which she then falls 'that it seemed as if his very breath, warm and loving, fanned her cheeks from those walls', walls which bear the sacred imprint of his poetic pencillings (12–13). The poet himself, however, manages to avoid all her attempts to engineer a meeting and eventually commits suicide in despair at never finding the 'unattainable creature' of his dreams, the 'undiscoverable, elusive' inspiration of his last volume, 'Lyrics to a Woman Unknown'. As a final irony, Ella herself dies in giving birth to a child who, by an 'inexplicable trick of nature', bears 'strong traces of resemblance' to the poet (25). There has, of course, been no actual relationship between them. However impossible the final genetic twist may be, the story illustrates how little the erotic need involve relationship with a 'real' object.

Another of *Life's Little Ironies* takes place 'On the Western Circuit' where a London barrister, eyeing the various 'gyrating personages' flashing 'kaleidoscopically' past on a circus hobbyhorse with 'long plate-glass mirrors set at angles', selects with some difficulty 'the prettiest girl out of the several pretty ones revolving' and studies her 'as well as he was able during each of her brief transits across his visual field'. She meanwhile feels herself to be 'the fixed point in an undulating, dazzling, lurid universe' in which he 'loomed forward most prominently' (85–6), a description which is confirmed as a metaphor for the human condition – the impossibility, in particular, of direct undistorted relationship – in a sentence which reads like a parody of Hardy:

> Each time that she approached the half of her orbit that lay nearest him they gazed at each other with smiles, and with that unmistakable expression which means so little at the moment, yet so often leads up to passion, heartache, union, disunion, devotion, overpopulation, drudgery, content, resignation, despair. (87)

Here, compressed into two lines, are the results of relations between the sexes as Hardy sees them.

This whole performance is observed from a window overlooking the square by a lady of about thirty, 'what is called an interesting creature rather than a handsome woman', who turns out to be the young girl's mistress. She was made a widow for the magazine serial, her husband being restored to her among other changes in the final version (Page, 1977: 128). When she comes to collect her maid, the crowd presses her so close to the barrister that 'his breath fanned her cheek', while he, taking advantage of the situation, clasps her hand, clearly under the impression that it is the girl's, and, finding no resistance, slips 'two of his fingers inside her glove, against her palm' (*LLI*: 89). Fascinated by a combination of his gentlemanly manners and seeming sexual sophistication (she finds him 'very wicked and nice'), she relapses into Bovarine ennui, 'lonely impressionable creature that she was', regretting that she had not married 'a London man who knew the subtleties of love-making as they were evidently known to him who had mistakenly caressed her hand' (91).

The barrister meanwhile indulges his 'violent fancy' for the girl, wins her 'body and soul' and immediately loses interest, returning to London with a sense of relief. Distance and the monotony of his work combine to reawaken his desire but when a letter arrives from the maid he delays opening it, partly for the same erotic reason that the 'Imaginative Woman' postponed her enjoyment of the photograph, but also because he feels his own 'imaginative sentiment' is more likely to satisfy his desire than her writing. It turns out, however, to be 'the most charming little missive he had ever received from woman' (note the generic term) and he enters into a passionate correspondence, unaware that it is not the maid who replies, since she is illiterate, but the mistress, 'possessed to the bottom of her soul with the image of a man to whom she was hardly so much as a name'. His looks, his voice, his 'tender touch' and finally his successful seduction of another woman in a mere two days have an irresistible 'fascination for her as a she-animal' (97). This last 'crowning' attribute, together with a sentence describing the mistress as 'a woman whose deeper nature had never been stirred', does not appear in the manuscript or serial versions of the story, Hardy allowing himself to add such unacceptably explicit recognitions of female sexuality in the final process of revision.

The mistress's 'predilection' for the barrister, she recognises, is 'subtle and imaginative', synonyms again for unreal, but this does not prevent her from living in an 'ecstasy of fancy' (99) until faced with the dilemma of his proposal which she advises the now pregnant maid to accept. After the wedding, aware of his mistake, the barrister extracts one kiss from the mistress, with the injunction: 'If it was all pure invention in those letters, give me your cheek only. If you meant what you said, let it be lips', before he resigns himself to a marriage as 'a galley, in which he . . . was chained to work for the rest of his life' with no compensation but the rereading of 'all those sweet letters . . . signed "Anna"' (105–7). I have refrained from giving any names until now, partly because the story is not about characters in the conventional sense but about erotic images produced by fertile imaginations. The 'Anna' the barrister loves does not exist: she is a combination of the visual image encountered on the hobbyhorse and the signature on the letters.

These last two stories in particular, extravagant though they are in terms of plot, explore with sympathetic irony the irrational world of unsatisfied desire. Clearly unfulfilled by their marriages, the wives throw themselves wholeheartedly into erotic fantasy until it dominates their lives. To call such fantasy 'unreal' is to miss the point that it becomes the most 'real' element in their respective worlds.

## A CHANGED MAN

The full title of Hardy's final volume of short stories, *A Changed Man, The Waiting Supper, and Other Tales, Concluding with The Romantic Adventures of a Milkmaid*, has been seen, 'by the absence of any thematic concept', to embody an 'admission that the book has no coherent unifying principle' (Brady, 1982: 157). Yet the same distorting processes of desire, increased by the distance, difference and inaccessibility of its object and diminished by actual contact, can be observed in many of these tales, particularly those included in the title. Other stories, such as 'Enter a Dragoon', in which a woman treasures her fiancé's memory only to discover his widow tending his grave, illustrate the illusory nature of love, while 'What the Shepherd Saw', like a machine on a seaside arcade, presents four different moonlit encounters which are tragically misinterpreted by a jealous husband. Five of the twelve stories, written between 1881 and 1900, warrant more detailed discussion.

'A Changed Man' itself is told from the perspective of a voyeur, a

man with an oriel window overlooking the High Street in Casterbridge, who observes a local girl's fascination with the Hussars in
general and a handsome captain in particular, a man with 'an
attractive hint of wickedness in his manner which was sure to
make him adorable with good young women' (*CM*: 4). Attending
their wedding, he jots in his prayer book a somewhat ominous
verse which begins and ends with the lines:

> If hours be years, the twain are blest,
> For now they solace sweet desire. [8]

But hours are not years, and in the course of time the handsome
young captain is transformed into an earnest, dull clergyman who
drives his wife into a 'reckless flirtation' with a young lieutenant.
When the husband dies in a valiant attempt to combat cholera the
lieutenant duly proposes, though 'there was languor in his utterance, hinting at the probability that it was perfunctorily made'
(22). They never, in fact, marry, for which the narrator posits a
number of possible reasons:

> whether because the obstacle had been the source of love, or
> from a sense of error, and because Mrs. Maumbry bore a less
> attractive look as a widow than before, their feelings seemed to
> decline from their former incandescence to a mere tepid civility.
> (23)

Desire, it seems, can die as perversely and unpredictably as it
rises.

'The Waiting Supper' begins with an erotic scene typical of
Hardy: a young farmer gazing through the lighted window of a
manor-house at the object of his desire within. She soon escapes
to meet him secretly in the garden, as she has done for the past
three years, though she continues to urge him to travel abroad and
become a more acceptable suitor in her father's eyes. She explains
somewhat tactlessly why his absence would be preferable to his
presence for her as well: 'The realities would not stare at us so. You
would be a pleasant dream to me, which I would be free to indulge
in without reproach to my conscience' (31). She is plainly tiring of
the simple farmer who presents a 'romantic object for a woman's
dream' only when 'idealised by moonlight, or a thousand miles of

distance' (42). Seeing him dance with the dairyman's daughter momentarily rekindles her desire, but when this last flickering of her love subsides the young man decides to leave. He returns fifteen years later to find her abandoned by her explorer-husband, whose possible return prevents their ever marrying. Possession is indefinitely postponed although the farmer visits the object of his desire on a daily basis, moving to a cottage only five hundred yards away, which provides sufficient distance to keep his desire warm without exhausting his energy. Even when the belated discovery of the husband's death leaves them free to marry, the couple decide against it, having found the perfect arrangement for the perpetuation of desire.

'Alicia's Diary' tells a morbid tale of rivalry between two sisters ended only by the suicide by drowning of the object of their desire. The heroine of 'A Mere Interlude' has better luck, though her first husband, married on impulse while waiting for the ferry to take her to an arranged wedding with an older man, is also drowned. As she ponders what to do, 'his image, in her mind's eye, waned curiously, receded far away, grew stranger and stranger, less and less real' (273). So she returns to the older man, goes ahead with the marriage and eventually enjoys a relationship based upon friendship rather than desire. She has to endure a macabre honeymoon, sleeping between her living husband in one room and the corpse of her dead one in the next, but the point is that her short-lived romance becomes a mere 'fantasy' (275) in comparison with the daily routine of her second marriage, which abandons the dangerous currents of desire. The erotic and the everyday are two separate worlds.

The final tale in this volume, 'The Romantic Adventures of a Milkmaid', gives more weight to the attractions of the erotic, the exotic and the unfamiliar. The eponymous milkmaid, engaged though she is to a worthy young lime-burner, cannot reconcile herself to a life of drudgery once she has encountered a mysterious handsome baron whom she accompanies to a ball, for which she undergoes a magic transformation, changing into a magnificent dress in a hollow elm in the centre of a dark wood. The images she imbibes at the ball, 'whirling figures . . . reflected from a glassy floor' (333), continue to occupy her mind, preventing her from paying any attention to her lime-burner until he turns in despair to the baron, who guiltily provides the kind of glamorous furniture to which the milkmaid now aspires. Some magnificent mirrors make her cry with joy, 'I can see myself in a hundred places' (342).

But the lonely baron also dwells on 'her image' (347) and summons her once more to a meeting for which she misses her wedding. The steadfast lime-burner continues nevertheless to pursue her, even courting another woman in an attempt to 'warm' her up. He finally succeeds, in spite of a late bid by the baron to escape with the milkmaid in his yacht. The tale ends with her confessing to her husband the fascination the baron still holds for her. Hardy's own copy of the story contains a note dated 1927 to the effect that 'the ending originally sketched' involved her 'disappearing with the baron in his yacht . . . and being no more heard of in England' (Brady, 1982: 168–9). Either way, it dramatises once more the unpredictability of desire and its undermining of the everyday world. It also illustrates to what extent the erotic is a matter of images, both of the self and of the other, images which are far removed from 'reality'.

Nothing is as it seems in the world of Hardy's short stories. Even the most seemingly innocent among them such as 'Our Exploits at West Poley', ostensibly about some children who succeed in diverting a stream at its secret underground source, turns out to be susceptible to a sexual reading. As the fictitious founder of the Alternative Centre for Thomas Hardy Studies points out, this story reaches its climax

> when the two pre-pubescent males find themselves lost and drowning in the cave, itself screened and fringed by bushes, with nothing to help them but a small supply of inadequate guttering candles. (Jacobson, 1984: 178)

One of them insists on climbing into an 'arched nook' tantalisingly out of their reach, but the other realises that it would not 'look so wonderful if we got close to it'. The reality of sex, in other words, proves more frightening and less alluring than the delights of the erotic imagination.

None of these stories, it should be noted, concerns itself very deeply with characterisation in the conventional sense, which may explain their relative unpopularity. What they do show, in a complex and often powerful manner, is the perennial perversity of desire: its refusal to accommodate itself to morality, to marriage, to any of the means by which people try to bring their lives under some form of control. The world Hardy depicts in his short stories is anarchic and fundamentally cruel, for desire is seen to bring in its wake suffering, sadness and a total disregard for the conventions by which society struggles to survive. To repress it is dangerous and debilitating, yet to indulge it is to make the everyday world which we call 'real' meaningless and absurd.

# 7

# *Tess of the d'Urbervilles*: A Pure Woman?

The erotic world of Hardy's fiction has so far been found to contain little in the way of purity. It will not therefore be surprising that the subtitle, 'A Pure Woman', added to the first edition of *Tess* but absent from the expurgated, more conventionally decent serial version of the novel, was part of a wider campaign to challenge such contemporary values which involved Hardy in a number of late manuscript alterations (Laird, 1975: 100; Grindle, 1983: 37). Many critics have balked at attributing purity to a fornicator, unmarried mother, religious sceptic, adulterer and murderess (Blake, 1982: 690), but Hardy renewed the attack in the preface to the 'fifth' edition, accusing such critics of

> an inability to associate the idea of the subtitle adjective with any but the artificial and derivative meaning which has resulted to it from the ordinances of civilization. They ignore the meaning of the word in Nature, together with all aesthetic claims upon it, not to mention the spiritual interpretation afforded by the finest side of their own Christianity. (*Tess*: 29–30)

Tess, in other words, is purely natural and purely woman (the essence of the feminine), pure in beauty and in her motives. Hardy conceded in conversation with Edmund Blunden that she lost 'a certain purity in her last fall', in returning to Alec, but insisted nevertheless that she retained her 'innate purity' in spite of her traumatic sexual experiences (Blunden, 1941: 79).

Hardy's preface claims that the novel says 'something more in fiction than had been said' before, giving expression to 'tacit opinion' rather than 'the merely vocal formulae of society', embodying 'views of life prevalent at the end of the nineteenth century' (*Tess*: 29–30). He is clearly aware of the 'potentially subversive' nature of entering 'areas of experience hitherto fenced off because of the explosive material apprehended as buried there' (Stewart, 1971: 164). He continues, as we shall see, to write indirectly rather than openly about subconscious drives only beginning to be recognised, 'the necessary laws of loving' as outlined by Freud. But in presenting Tess as a victim of male splitting of women (Angel idealising and Alec debasing her) and of a perpetual and inescapable struggle between nature and civilisation, Hardy points to similar phenomena as those described more 'scientifically' by Freud.

At the height of the controversy over his 'Tessimism' Hardy defined his understanding of tragedy in these terms, as 'the WORTHY encompassed by the INEVITABLE' (*Life*: 265). The novel portrays not only Tess but also her fellow-milkmaids, all infatuated with Angel Clare, as victims of irresistible drives common to their whole sex and race:

> They writhed feverishly under the oppressiveness of an emotion thrust on them by Nature's law – an emotion which they had neither expected nor desired. . . . The differences which distinguished them as individuals were abstracted by this passion, and each was but portion of one organism called sex. . . . The full recognition of the futility of their infatuation, from a social point of view; its purposeless beginning; its self-bounded outlook; its lack of everything to justify its exist- ence in the eye of civilization (while lacking nothing in the eye of Nature); the one fact that it did exist, ecstasizing them to a killing joy; all this imparted to them a resignation, a dignity, which a practical and sordid expectation of winning him as a husband would have destroyed. (*Tess*: 187)

It is a paragraph which virtually summarises the novel, encapsu- lating Tess's tragic and passionate struggle to reconcile the demands of nature and civilisation.

Tess, of course, is more the object than the subject of desire, a victim of male visions of that sexual 'succulence' of which contem- porary critics complained (Laird, 1975: 11). Not only in the eyes of the characters but in those of the narrator, more recent critics have agreed, she is altogether too edible, 'an object of the reader's consumption' (Goode, 1979: 102). Readers of this novel more than any other seem to divide along sexual lines, male critics too often repeating the mistakes of the male characters and falling in love with an image of their construction. 'Is it not . . . the strong, passionate, impure Tess we understand and love?' asks one disbeliever in her purity (Davis, 1968: 400). Feminist critics, on the other hand, have found 'an unusually overt maleness in the narrative voice':

> Time and again the narrator seeks to enter Tess, through her eyes – 'his [eyes] plumbed the ever-varying pupils, with their radiating fibrils of blue, and black, and gray, and violet' (p.198) – and through her flesh – 'as the day wears on its feminine smoothness is scarified by the stubble, and bleeds' (p.117). The phallic imagery of pricking, piercing and penetration which has been repeatedly noted, serves not only to create an image-chain linking Tess's experiences from the death of Prince to her final penetrative act of retaliation, but also to satisfy the narrator's fascination with the interiority of her sexuality, and his desire to take possession of her. (Boumelha, 1982: 120)

At the beginning of the novel the narrator hides behind a few passing 'strangers' who 'would look long at her in casually passing by, and grow momentarily fascinated by her freshness' to excuse the detail in which he describes Tess's physical charms. He even dwells on her lips when supposedly describing her accent, the characteristic intonation 'approximately rendered by the syllable UR':

> The pouted-up deep red mouth to which this syllable was native had hardly as yet settled into its definite shape, and her lower lip had a way of thrusting the middle of her top one upward, when they closed together after a word.

The narrator, then, is at least as interested in the shape of her lips as in the words they utter. He stresses, however, that not only as a subject but as an object, the image she presents is neither coherent or unified:

> Phases of her childhood lurked in her aspect still. As she walked along today, for all her bouncing handsome womanliness, you could sometimes see her twelfth year in her cheeks, or her ninth

sparkling from her eyes; and even her fifth would flit over the curves of her mouth now and then. (*Tess*: 42–3)

The narrator, it needs to be recognised, is interested in Tess as both subject and object. He notices, with male eyes and customary euphemistic circumlocution, the size of her breasts (being accused by contemporaries of indecent directness in this respect). But he notices too the failure of her body to express her feelings. 'One day she was pink and flawless; another pale and tragical', he writes of her last days at Marlott before leaving for Talbothays: 'When she was pink she was feeling less than when pale; her more perfect beauty accorded with her less elevated mood; her more intense mood with her less perfect beauty' (140). The 'dominant scopic regime of the novel' may at times reveal the narrator to be 'the speaking subject, the one whose desires structure our view of Tess' (Silverman, 1984: 10, 21). But the narrator also claims the right to speak for Tess, to enter her subjective consciousness and its struggle both to express her own feelings and to escape the imprisoning objectification of male desire.

From the passing strangers at the beginning of the novel to the sixteen patient policemen who wait for her to awake at Stonehenge at its end, Tess is the object of the erotic male gaze, which 'never innocently alights on its object' but 'constructs it in the image of its own desires' (7). Her body is the pure blank surface on which men inscribe or trace a variety of patterns, from Alec's coarse design to Angel's more ethereal portrait. There is a whole chain of related metaphors involving 'the tracing of a pattern, the making of a mark, the carving of a line or sign, and the act of writing', all of which embody a recognition of the way men 'write' women, inscribing their deepest needs on this beautiful surface (Miller, 1982: 118).

It is part of Tess's tragedy that her history is written, her identity formed, by the wrong man. She is first seen by Angel Clare, whose 'eyes lighted' on her only at the end of the dance on Marlott Green, just as he has to hurry away (*Tess*: 45). It is left therefore to Alec d'Urberville to construct her in his more brutal fashion. His 'bold rolling eye' immediately settles on his pretty cousin at their first meeting (68), when his forcing of a strawberry through her reluctantly parted lips signals quite clearly his designs upon her. For the moment, however, he is content merely to watch 'her pretty and unconscious munching', fascinated by the same physical development which attracted the passing strangers:

She had an attribute which amounted to a disadvantage just now; and it was this that caused Alec d'Urberville's eyes to rivet themselves upon her. It was a luxuriance of aspect, a fullness of growth, which made her appear more of a woman than she really was. (71)

The episode ends with the narrator ruminating ominously on her being 'doomed to be seen and coveted that day by the wrong man', her destiny decided by an accident of timing (72).

At their next encounter in the gig, when Alec frightens Tess into holding his waist, bargaining for a kiss as the price for slowing down, it is made even clearer that he is attempting to stamp her with his own desire. She finally agrees to the kiss and he is 'on the point of imprinting the desired salute' when she dodges aside. The 'kiss of mastery' to which she eventually submits, however, causes her to flush with shame and 'unconsciously' to remove 'the spot on her cheek that had been touched by his lips' (85). His 'imprint' is clearly felt as a 'stain', her reluctance to accept his intimacies being increased as part of the late revision of the manuscript. She had earlier been presented as more naive and trusting, allowing Alec to kiss her four times and showing none of the 'fire' with which she now expresses her anger at Alec's trick, nor the 'defiant laugh' at the success of her own manoeuvre, losing her hat in order to escape from the gig (Jacobus, 1976: 326–7). Even her anger, however, is portrayed in an erotic light, for it leaves her 'face on fire' while the act of opening her mouth to say 'no' merely inflames him further by revealing 'the red and ivory' within (*Tess*: 86). What Tess says carries little weight against what Alec sees in her.

The most indelible mark inscribed by Alec upon Tess's body, of course, occurs in The Chase. Even his fingers disfigure her pure body and sink 'into her as into down' (106). She is once more surrounded by symbols of masculine strength and natural fecundity, 'the primeval yews and oaks', their 'roosting birds' and their 'hopping rabbits and hares'. The natural context of this decisive event runs completely contrary to the 'civilized' morality which causes an 'immeasurable social chasm . . . to divide our heroine's personality' from her earlier innocent self. The narrator asks, without hope of adequate answer,

Why it was that upon this beautiful feminine tissue, sensitive as gossamer, and practically blank as snow as yet, there should have been traced such a coarse pattern as it was doomed to receive. (107)

Tess herself, for the narrator at least, remains as pure as her skin, for the coarse pattern is not of her design.

What precisely is supposed to have happened in The Chase is left tantalisingly vague and unclear. Tess later reproaches herself for her 'weakness', telling Alec that 'My eyes were dazed by you for a little', implying at least some willingness and responsibility on her part (112). It is, in Hardy's terms, a tribute to her beauty that his desire to leave his mark on her remains alive even after possession. He demands a final kiss:

She thereupon turned and lifted her face to his, and remained like a marble term while he imprinted a kiss upon her cheek – half perfunctorily, half as if zest had not yet quite died out. (113)

At this point the manuscript initially continued: 'for only a month had elapsed since she had ceased to defend herself against him' (Laird, 1975: 72), which suggests force on his part. But this too is ambiguous, the main point seeming to be that he might have been more 'zestful' had the interval been longer. Tess meanwhile rests her eyes 'upon the remotest trees . . . as though she were nearly unconscious of what he did'. She remains entirely passive, turning her head for him to kiss the other cheek, which feels 'damp and smoothly chill as the skin of the mushrooms in the fields around' (*Tess*: 113). The narrative consciousness, as so often, identifies with the male point of view, the desiring subject, even to the feel of her cheeks. But Tess remains pure, associated with sculpted artefacts and other objects of natural beauty.

When Tess confesses to her mother, in a passage added in 1892, to a 'confused surrender' to the 'adroit advantages he took of her helplessness', having been 'blinded by his ardent manners' but then having 'suddenly despised and disliked him', her complicity in her downfall seems clear enough. Her mother, however, draws a similar conclusion to the narrator (even if her theology is different): "Tis nater, after all, and what do please God!' (117; see Laird, 1975: 176–7). One of the field-women confuses her 'surrender' still further in another 1892 addition: 'A little more than persuading had to do wi' the coming o't' (126; see Brady, 1986: 132–3). Whatever the 'truth' of the matter – and Hardy himself seems never finally to have decided – the narrative continues to stress Tess's oneness with nature throughout. Her guilty con- science, which makes her see the rain as nature weeping over her folly, is seen to be a 'mistaken creation' of her fancy, not an integral part of her consciousness. It is a cultural product, an intertextual artefact, 'based on shreds of convention, peopled by phantoms and voices antipathetic to her':

It was they that were out of harmony with the actual world, not she. Walking among the sleeping birds in the hedges, watching the skipping rabbits on a moonlit warren, or standing under a pheasant-laden bough, she looked upon herself as a figure of Guilt intruding into the haunts of Innocence. But all the while she was making a distinction where there was no difference. Feeling herself in antagonism she was quite in accord. She had been made to break an accepted social law, but no law known to the environment in which she fancied herself such an anomaly. (121)

Tess herself, misled by social conventions, fails to recognise the extent to which her actions have been 'purely' natural.

This oneness with nature is presented as a particularly female characteristic, part of Tess's being 'purely' woman. In binding the corn during harvest, the narrator insists, a woman

becomes part and parcel of outdoor nature, and is not merely an object set down therein as at ordinary times. A field-man is a personality afield; a field-woman is a portion of the field; she has somehow lost her own margin, imbibed the essence of her surrounding, and assimilated herself with it. (123)

Tess, too, in helping with the harvest, loses her superficial cultural 'personality', mingling with the deeper forces of nature as in the sexual act itself. She is depicted 'holding the corn in an embrace like that of a lover' while the 'feminine smoothness' of her unprotected skin, in one of the phallic images already noted, 'becomes scarified by the stubble and bleeds' (124). As she continues to help with the harvest she recovers confidence in her own 'innate sensations' as opposed to the 'conventional' feelings responsible for her misery (127). Her beauty as she baptises her dying baby is 'immaculate' (130). Her strength and health too survive even its death. For, as she comes to recognise, 'the recuperative power which pervades organic nature was surely not denied to maidenhood alone'. The return of spring moves her, 'as it moved other wild animals', bringing with it a resurgence of the pleasure principle, 'the invincible instinct towards self-delight' (119–20). She travels to Talbothays with renewed vigour which finds expression in the familiar words of the psalms praising all living things upon earth, transformed on her lips into a pagan celebration of the 'forces of out-door Nature' (141).

In moving to Talbothays, then, as well as in falling in love there, Tess is seen to be in tune with natural forces deeper than conventional social morality. Her first sight of Angel Clare stirs subliminal memories whose meaning 'suddenly flashed upon her' (149), a sense shared more feebly by Clare, who is unable to recall where he met her. The force of this repetition has been likened to Freud's analysis of 'hysterical trauma':

For Freud, the first episode is sexual but not understood as such at the time. The second event is innocuous, but is experienced as a repetition of the first, liberating its traumatic effect. (Miller, 1982: 136)

Tess, so innocent of her sexual nature on their first encounter, now experiences a 'flood of memory' which her more recent experiences help to explain (*Tess*: 149). Angel, observing her closely at breakfast and discerning in her 'a fresh and virginal daughter of Nature', is also transported 'into a joyous and unforeseeing past'. It is ominous, however, that he should spend so much time observing and 'regarding her', forcing her to behave 'with the constraint of a domestic animal that perceives itself to be watched' (158). For the scopic drive can be seen to dominate Angel as it dominated Alec, causing him also to create her in the image of his desire.

For a time, though, the two lovers inhabit an Edenic world of unrestrained natural instincts. The garden through which Tess creeps as 'stealthily as a cat' to listen 'like a fascinated bird' to Angel's harp 'had been left uncultivated for some years' and is now 'rank with juicy grass which sent up mists of pollen'. Her pure limbs are once more marked and stained with entirely natural deposits as she gathers

cuckoo-spittle on her skirts, cracking snails that were underfoot,
staining her hands with thistle-milk and slug-slime, and rub-
bing off upon her naked arms sticky blights which, though
snow-white on the apple-tree trunks, made madder stains on
her skin. (161–2)

'Madder' stains, of course, are bright red, 'blood-red' in the
manuscript, part of a web of red imagery pervading the novel,
indicative of both the beauty and the suffering of nature (Miller,
1982: 123).

Angel and Tess are seen gradually to converge 'under an
irresistible law, as surely as two streams in one vale' (*Tess*: 168).
Isolated in the early hours of the morning, they feel 'as if they were
Adam and Eve', or even the new Adam in the hour of resurrection
with the Magdalen by his side. Tess once again merges with all
women to become 'a visionary essence of woman – a whole sex
condensed into one typical form' (170). She needs no artificial
decoration: 'diamonds of moisture from the mist' hang from her
eyelashes 'and drops upon her hair, like seed pearls' (171). She is
at her most beautiful in natural settings, as when Angel observes
her in the dairy with the sun shining 'upon her pink-gowned form
and her white curtain-bonnet, and upon her profile, rendering it
keen as a cameo cut from the dun background of the cow'. The
narrative dwells on his response:

> How very lovable her face was to him. . . . And it was in her
> mouth that this culminated. Eyes almost as deep and speaking
> he had seen before, and cheeks perhaps as fair; brows as arched,
> a chin and throat almost as shapely; her mouth he had seen
> nothing to equal on the face of the earth. To a young man with
> the least fire in him that little upward lift in the middle of her
> red top lip was distracting, infatuating, maddening. (190)

It is difficult to tell whether this is Angel's self-justification (a form
of *erlebte Rede*) or the narrator's male sympathy. Either way, Angel
spends so much time studying the 'curves of those lips' that he can
'reproduce them mentally with ease' (191). On this occasion he
jumps up from his seat, goes quickly towards 'the desire of his
eyes' and clasps her in his arms. Tess's response is relatively
subdued, toned down in the process of purifying revision. In the

manuscript she 'panted' and 'burst into a succession of quick sobs'. In the text as it now stands she merely 'sank upon him in her momentary joy, with something like an ecstatic cry' (Jacobus, 1976: 330). It is altogether more sedate, but still unquestionably sexual.

Tess continues to be seen very much as a part of nature, a warm-blooded animal. When Angel surprises her yawning he sees the 'red interior of her mouth as if it had been a snake's', admires the 'satin delicacy' of her skin and finds her the embodiment of 'pure' and natural sexuality:

> The brim-fulness of her nature breathed from her. It was a moment when a woman's soul is more incarnate than at any other time; when the most spiritual beauty bespeaks itself flesh; and sex takes the outside place in the presentation.

The purity of her incarnate soul does not involve a disembodied spirituality; it is expressed in physical beauty which Angel clearly longs to possess, like the penetrating male sun which he feels

> slanting in by the window upon his back, as he held her tightly to his breast; upon her inclining face, upon the blue veins of her temple, upon her naked arm, and her neck, and into the depths of her hair.

She is purely a natural creature, 'warm as a sunned cat', regarding him 'as Eve at her second waking might have regarded Adam', while he longs yet again to enter her mysterious depths, to plumb the 'deepness' of her 'ever-varying pupils' (*Tess*: 210).

Their love-making at the dairy continues to be depicted as purely natural. When they skim the milk together he cleans her finger 'in nature's way' (211). When they break up the curds, against whose 'immaculate whiteness' Tess's hands display 'the pinkness of the rose', Angel takes advantage of her sleeves being rolled 'far above the elbow' to kiss 'the inside vein of her soft arm'. And though her arm, like the cheek Alec kissed, feels 'as cold and damp ... as a new-gathered mushroom', her accelerated pulse drives the blood to her 'finger-ends, and the cool arms flushed hot' (217). When they drive together to deliver the milk to the railway station, where she stands with 'rainy face and hair' in 'the suspended attitude of a friendly leopard at pause', bewildered by

the advance of civilisation and asking innocent questions about
the sophisticated Londoners (228), she proves her love in the way
that comes naturally to her:

> She clasped his neck, and for the first time Clare learnt what an
> impassioned woman's kisses were like upon the lips of one
> whom she loved with all her heart and soul, as Tess loved him.
> (231)

Her consent to marriage comes as a final victory for those natural
instincts which obey the pleasure principle above all else, that
'"appetite for joy" which pervades all creation' (232), and nature is
seen once more to triumph over civilisation.

It becomes increasingly evident, however, that Angel's love for
Tess is not so purely natural. The narrator, even at the height of
their passion, calls him 'more spiritual than animal',

> less Byronic than Shelleyan; could love desperately, but with a
> love more especially inclined to be imaginative and ethereal; it
> was a fastidious emotion which could jealously guard the loved
> one against his very self. (234)

'Imaginative and ethereal' are alterations in the manuscript which
emphasise the erotic, cultural, unnatural elements in Angel's
affection. Again, even as he hastens the preparations for their
wedding, it is stressed that he loves her 'rather ideally and
fancifully than with the impassioned thoroughness of her feeling
for him' (245). Tess herself, kneeling in her room before their
departure from Talbothays, is frightened both by the depth of her
own love and by the unreal elements she detects in his idealisation
of her, 'for she you love is not my real self, but one in my image;
the one I might have been' (256). After their marriage but before
her confession he is depicted as 'looking at her silently' as if
'deciding on the true construction of a difficult passage', unsure
how to read her properly (260). And when she finally tells him of
the events at Trantridge he positively denies that she is the same
person as the one he had loved: 'You were one person; now you
are another' (271). He sees her for the first time 'without irradiation' while she tries to convince him that it 'is in your own mind
what you are angry at' (274).

What Tess's confession does, in fact, is 'to call into question the absolute authority of his gaze to construct her' and to disclose 'the gap separating desire from the ostensible object' (Silverman, 1984: 14). He is forced to acknowledge that her eyes could be 'seeing another world' to his (*Tess*: 278). She continues to look 'absolutely pure' (280) and to love him with perfect Pauline charity (274). But she is no longer the ideal image he had painted her, 'so pure, so sweet, so virginal' (277), the word 'virginal' being new in the first edition (Laird, 1975: 171). The 'fifth' edition drives home Hardy's increased anger at his character's (and his critics') refusal to accept the purely natural:

> *Some might risk the odd paradox that with more animalism he would have been the nobler man. We do not say it.* Yet Clare's love was *doubtless* ethereal to a fault, imaginative to impracticality. With these natures, corporeal presence is something less appealing than corporeal absence, the latter creating an ideal presence that conveniently drops the defects of the real. . . . The figurative phrase was true: she was another woman than the one who had excited his desire. (287; see Laird, 1975: 136, with the words added in 1892 in italics)

That Angel's rejection of the 'un-intact' Tess involves a repression of his own 'natural' feelings emerges quite clearly in the sleep-walking sequence in which he manages to 'negotiate the dangers of turbulent water', symbolising the raging passions beneath, in order to lay her body in the empty stone coffin of the Abbey-church, thereby burying the sexual instinct (Tanner, 1968: 229). Tess derives some comfort from the fact that his subconscious self still recognises her as his wife, but is frightened to wake him lest his 'daytime aversion' recur (*Tess*: 292). She refrains the following morning from telling him of the escapade since it would only 'anger him . . . to know that he had instinctively manifested a fondness for her of which his commonsense did not approve' (294). Angel accordingly remains firmly under the control of his unbending conscience or superego, which occupies 'the remote depths of his constitution' as 'a hard logical deposit, like a vein of metal in a soft loam' (284). Completely out of touch with his deeper feelings, he allows her to return to her parents 'and hardly knew that he loved her still' (298). Her 'cooing voice' continues to haunt his night-time consciousness, when he can still feel 'the velvet touch of her lips' and 'the warmth of her breath' (309). He insists to his parents that she is indeed spotless while the terms of his proposal to Izz Huet show that he is already beginning to question the values of the 'civilization' that would condemn it, 'Western civilization that is' (315).

Angel's departure exposes Tess once more to the dangers of the male-dominated world in which she is reduced to an erotic and economic object. Nature now reveals its harsh side in the form of the wounded pheasants, so 'unmannerly' treated by the hunters, whom she puts out of their misery. In comparison with these, she realises, her own suffering appears slight, 'based on nothing more tragic than a sense of condemnation under an arbitrary law of society which had no foundation in Nature' (324). She resolves nevertheless to reduce her attractiveness as an object of male lust, clipping her eyebrows and covering her face with a handkerchief. Even the landscape she traverses, however, is sexualised, 'bosomed with semi-globular tumuli' (326). Flintcomb Ash itself is covered with 'myriads of loose white flints in bulbous, cusped, and phallic shapes' at which Marian shrieks with laughter while Tess remains 'severely obtuse' (331–3).

Try as she may to resist and to repress her sexuality, Tess cannot escape her role as an object of erotic fascination. When she stumbles on Alec at his preaching she observes the 'electric' effect she still has on him. She immediately turns to go, only to feel his 'fancied gaze' on her back (353). He, of course, pursues her and continues to fix his eyes upon her, 'contemplating her' (356). He complains of being unable to rid himself of her 'image' (368), confessing to a 'burning desire' to see the woman he once despised but who remained 'unsmirched in spite of all'. He no longer, in Freudian terms, debases her but he continues to blame her for her beauty: 'never was such a maddening mouth since Eve's' (370). He casts himself in the role of Satan, complete with fork, coming to tempt Eve in her parents' allotment and she falls a second time, returning to live with him in repayment for his kindness to her family. Having killed him, she enjoys a brief taste of paradise with Angel which is described in purely natural terms, as on the morning when they are discovered by the cleaning lady, her 'lips being parted like a half-open flower near his cheek' (442). Nothing, it appears, can sully her innate natural purity.

Tess dies, at the end of the novel, a victim of fate, of civilisation, and above all of male desire, having learnt 'the cruelty of lust and the fragility of love' (326). She never fully succeeds in becoming a subject rather than an object. In many of the most important scenes in the novel, it has been pointed out, her

> consciousness is all but edited out. Tess is asleep, or in a reverie, at almost every crucial turn of the plot: at Prince's death, at the time of her seduction by Alec, when the sleepwalking Angel buries his image of her, at his return to find her at the Herons, and when the police take her at Stonehenge. (Boumelha, 1982: 121)

When she tries to speak to Angel, 'He silenced her by a kiss' (*Tess*: 256) and when she studies Alec too closely he exclaims, 'Don't look at me like that!' (356). Even the narrator, as we have seen, is often less concerned with what she says than with the shape of her lips. The texts, in fact, remain confused over her diction, varying between dialect and Standard English (Poole, 1981: 345). She is split partly by her education: having 'passed the Sixth Standard in the National School', she 'spoke two languages: the dialect at home, more or less; ordinary English abroad and to persons of quality' (*Tess*: 48). Later, of course, she picks up Clare's vocabulary and accent along with fragments of his knowledge.

But Tess is also split in the way Julia Kristeva argues all women are split: between desire and language, attempting to express their own subjectivity and sexuality in a language dominated by men (Kristeva, 1980: 237–43). She is split too by the two men, Angel and Alec, who idealise and debase her simultaneously, and by the narrator, who both describes her with erotic fascination and attempts to purify her. Even her two lips are made to speak different languages, the top one lifting invitingly when she smiles while the other remains 'severely still' (*Tess*: 161). Eventually, in a passage added in 1892, she disowns her body altogether, Clare recognising on his return that 'his original Tess had spiritually ceased to recognise the body before him as hers' (429). Her tragedy can in this sense be said to lie in her failure 'to *possess herself*, to make her body and the languages that it speaks her own' (Poole, 1981: 343). Her much-vaunted purity cannot prevent her image and eventually her body being appropriated by others.

# 8

# Sue Bridehead:
# A New Woman

Sue Bridehead is in many ways at the centre of *Jude the Obscure*. It has been argued that she 'takes the book away from the title character, because she is stronger, more complex, and more significant'. Her very inconsistency and elusiveness, the sense of profound depths lying beneath her 'brilliant and puzzling surface', create a fascinating 'air of the inexplicable and even the mysterious' (Heilman, 1966: 307). She is very much 'The New Woman', which is one of the titles Hardy himself proposed for a dramatisation of the novel (Millgate, 1971: 312). In her reading of Mill, Shelley and Swinburne, in her questioning of the institution of marriage, and above all in her search for a new model of womanhood, she fits the mould of the 'modern intelligent mentally emancipated young woman of cities' whom Hardy, writing of one of Florence Henniker's heroines, reckoned to be 'by far the most interesting type of femininity the world provides for man's eyes at the present day' (Blake, 1982: 147).

*'For man's eyes'*, notice; the more the New Woman attempts to escape the role of erotic object to which so many men reduce her, the more she succeeds only in provoking still more sexual interest, offering in addition to her other charms the challenge of a difficult conquest. As a pioneering feminist Sue Bridehead fails fully to overcome the problem of liberating herself from male expectations without repressing her own sexuality. As a late Victorian she finds herself torn between ascetic and hedonistic, Hebraic and Hellenistic, tendencies – unable to free herself, in spite of her 'mental emancipation', from a deeply ingrained fear of sexuality. As a fictional construct, moreover, she is portrayed mainly through men's eyes, as seen by the narrator, by Phillotson and, most of all, by Jude. To an unprecedented extent in his fiction Hardy allows the perspective of a single character to dominate the story, so that

Sue becomes 'enmeshed in Jude's limited point of view' (Langland, 1980: 12). Her own problems, therefore, are further compounded by his.

In spite of Hardy's many textual revisions – perhaps because of them – it is difficult to establish how far the narrator's perspective, and that of the author, are to be distanced from Jude's. The whole novel reflects Jude's view of sex, telling, in the words of the Preface, of the disasters 'that may press in the wake of the strongest passion known to humanity, . . . of a deadly war waged between flesh and spirit' (*Jude*: 23). For both Jude and the narrator sex is a destructive instinct, undermining man's 'higher' aspirations, while women are weak creatures, unable to think clearly or to carry out their convictions. All the girls in Melchester Training College 'bear the legend "The Weaker"' upon their faces 'as the penalty of the sex wherein they were moulded'. They are doomed, in addition, to years of 'injustice, loneliness, child-bearing, and bereavement' (161). It is to this combination of weakness and hardship that Jude attributes Sue's failure of nerve: 'Strange difference of sex, that time and circumstance, which enlarge the views of most men, narrow the views of women almost invariably' (419). The novel, however, is more complicated than this; Jude's judgement is not altogether to be trusted.

Jude suffers, for a start, from the familiar Victorian symptoms of psychical impotence, dividing women into two types, the 'coarse' and sensual Arabella, whom he can freely desire, and the 'ethereal' Sue, whom he respects and admires but desires only with difficulty, fearing to lose her affection by indulging his 'lower' appetites. His seduction by Arabella is presented as a terrible fall, his first encounter with her being a grotesque parody of Christ's baptism. His elevated thoughts of Christminster ('I'll be her beloved son, in whom she shall be well pleased') are crowned not by a descending dove but by a pig's pizzle (Lodge, 1981: 112). The charms of the woman responsible for bringing him so firmly down to earth are entirely physical. Arabella is 'a complete and substantial female animal, no more, no less', with 'a round and prominent bosom, full lips, perfect teeth, and the rich complexion of a Cochin hen's egg', and Jude singles her out from her companions by reciprocal desire, in Hardy's quaint circumlocution, 'in commonplace obedience to conjunctive orders from headquarters' (*Jude*: 58–9). The manuscript was originally more direct, referring to 'the authoritative operation of a natural law' (Boumelha, 1982: 146).

The point, however, is the same: nature, as always, proves stronger than culture.

Much of the critical outcry with which the novel was first received, the attacks on 'Jude the Obscene' and 'Hardy the Degenerate' (Millgate, 1982: 369), focused on this initial meeting with Arabella, which was much more explicit in the first edition. Later editions, from 1903 onwards, made much less play with the pig's 'characteristic part'. In the first edition, however,

> Jude held out his stick with the fragment of pig dangling therefrom, looking elsewhere the while, and faintly colouring.
>
>     She, too, looked in another direction, and took the piece as though ignorant of what her hand was doing. She hung it temporarily on the rail of the bridge, and then, by a species of mutual curiosity, they both turned, and regarded it. (*Jude*: 439)

In all versions it is clear that Arabella knows precisely what she is doing, turning 'her eyes critically upon him' out of 'amatory curiosity' while he responds 'against his intention – almost against his will' to 'the unvoiced call of woman to man'. Having never previously 'looked at a woman to consider her as such' he now makes up for lost time: 'He gazed from her eyes to her mouth, thence to her bosom, and to her full round naked arms, wet, mottled with the chill of the water, and firm as marble' (60–1). His personality has become split, part of him recognising that it 'had been no vestal who chose *that* missile for opening her attack on him', the rest being blinded by his new 'channel for emotional interest', previously sublimated in his work (62).

Arabella, then, and the degrading sexuality for which she stands, are responsible for seducing Jude from his studies. When he tries to read his New Testament he is drawn towards her as if 'a compelling arm of extraordinary muscular power' were dragging him 'towards the embrace of a woman for whom he had no respect'. When he arrives at her cottage he is struck by a strong 'smell of piggeries' (64). These unclean animals continue to dominate their courtship, for it is in pursuit of a pig that she warms up his appetite. They first dodge around the potatoes and cabbages, snatching kisses as they can. She then gives him 'her now hot hand' as they pursue the poor beast across the field until she gives up the chase in a conveniently isolated spot, flinging herself to the ground and pulling Jude down on top, 'her form heaving and falling in quick pants, her face flushed, her full red lips parted, and a fine dew of perspiration on her skin' (72), all indicating the strength of her sexual appetite. She later draws Jude on by means of a cochin's egg wrapped in a pig's bladder which she nurses in her bosom, explaining that 'it is natural for a woman to want to bring live things into the world' (75), which is precisely what they proceed to attempt for themselves, thereby giving credence to her later claims to be pregnant.

The sensual and, to Jude's mind, disgusting nature of his relationship with Arabella is reflected in this perpetual link between her and pigs. It is the botched killing of a pig which brings their marriage to a crisis and it is behind her father's squalid pork-butcher's shop that she captures him a second time (Lodge, 1981: 111). Her movements are always sexually suggestive, at least when reflected in the mirror of Jude's mind. It is in a mirror that he sees her practising her dimples and it is through a mirror that he observes her in the Christminster pub, tidying her hair and then lighting a customer's cigarette 'with ministering archness'. When she finally recognises Jude, the sexual suggestiveness of her posture is unambiguous: 'She idly allowed her fingers to rest on the pull of the beer-engine as she inspected him critically' (*Jude*: 199–201). Jude clearly feels both disgusted and judged by her demanding appetite, at once morally superior and sexually inadequate.

Sue Bridehead, in contrast, poses less of a physical threat, 'the delicate lines of her profile, and the small, tight, apple-like convexities of her bodice' being 'so different to Arabella's amplitudes' (207). Arabella's 'capacious bosom' (315), 'her breast's superb abundance' (334), remains a source of admiration and fear. But Sue presents a less imposing front, attracting Jude first as a bodiless photograph on his aunt's mantelpiece, 'a pretty girlish face, in a broad hat with radiating folds under the brim like the rays of a halo' (97). He invests this angelic image with powerful though unconscious desire, kissing the photograph 'he did not know why' (104–5). He visits her at work, retaining his incognito and feeling 'stimulated' by her presence. She remains for some time enigmatic, unknown, 'more or less an ideal character, about whose form he began to weave curious and fantastic day-dreams' (108), reflecting on the 'mystery' of her 'liquid, untranslatable eyes' long after a chance encounter as the 'bottled-up' emotion 'insensibly began to precipitate itself on this half-visionary form'

(109). He even follows her around the city, standing in wait for her by the cathedral at which she worships, a classic voyeur: 'To see her, and to be himself unseen and unknown, was enough for him at present' (111). When she finally appears, he remains 'throughout the service in a sustaining atmosphere of ecstasy' which, as the narrator wryly observes, 'blew as distinctly from Cyprus as from Galilee' (112).

The irony is, of course, that Venus dominates Sue's thoughts as much as Jude's. For while he attempts to disguise 'the real nature' of his feelings (112), idealising her as an angelic creature engaged in a 'sweet, saintly, Christian business' (108), she is struggling with sexual desires of her own. A significant flashback in the narrative underlines the difference between Sue Bridehead as the object of Jude's idealising desire and as the subject of her own contradictory impulses. The demure worshipper in the cathedral is shown recently to have purchased two large statues of Venus and Apollo, though they appear 'so very naked' once she has bought them that she covers them straight away with large leaves and passes them off to her landlady as St Peter and Mary Magdalene. In the secrecy of her room, however, 'at bedtime, when she was sure of being undisturbed', she unrobes them and places them, 'a candle on each side', on her chest of drawers while she reads first Gibbon and then Swinburne, her pagan rites contrasting with Jude's simultaneous mumbling of a passage from Paul's letter to the Corinthians, with its clear warnings against sexual temptation (115–16). Similarly, while Jude continues to imagine that the object of his erotic gaze in another church, with her 'pretty shoulders' and 'curiously nonchalant risings and sittings', would be horrified by the feelings which he now sees to be 'unmistakably of a sexual kind' if not quite the 'erotolepsy' of his lapse with Arabella (117–18), she takes the initiative to call upon him, displaying unmistakable sexual interest, looking him 'up and down curiously' (120) and falling well short of innocent frankness in describing the fate of her 'patron-saints' at the hands of her outraged landlady (123).

Jude's image of Sue is further complicated by seeing her succumb to Phillotson's advances, letting him place his arm around her waist under their umbrella, and by hearing from his aunt that she was never the paragon of modesty he imagined:

> Why, one day when she was walking into the pond with her
> shoes and stockings off, and her petticoats pulled above her

knees, afore I could cry out for shame, she said, 'Move on, aunty! This is no sight for modest eyes!' (130)

Like so many of Hardy's heroines she gains in erotic interest by being enigmatic, sexually alluring yet seemingly innocent as she holds his hand, 'dividing his fingers and coolly examining them, as if they were the fingers of a glove she was purchasing' (152). She becomes 'something of a riddle to him' (153), her conduct 'one lovely conundrum' (156), as she seems on the one hand to encourage his attentions and then to withdraw, suddenly embarrassed, for example, by the sight of her damp clothes spread out in his room. There is a suggestion of sexual ambivalence, too, in her appearance in Jude's clothes, looking as 'boyish as Ganymedes' and speaking with 'epicene tenderness' (173–4).

Sue's ambivalence, in fact, represents a deep split within herself. She wants to do what the 'boys do' (132), to be taken seriously in the world of men, and yet to retain her sexual difference. Her contradictoriness is not mere coquetry, for she is not an old-fashioned flirt, playing her lovers along, but a new-fangled feminist in a dilemma about her sexuality, not wanting to deny it but not wanting either to be reduced to a sexual object. This makes her appear, to men and even to modern feminists, inconsistent and perverse, 'by turns an enigma, a pathetic creature, a nut, and an iceberg' (Millet, 1977: 133). But her contradictoriness has 'depth and coherence' (Blake, 1983: 160), a coherence Hardy builds into the novel by allowing her to speak so much for herself. She rebels like Lyndall, the heroine of Olive Schreiner's *Story of a South African Farm*, against the notion that a woman must 'seem' and be silent, giving expression to all the aspirations of the New Woman, even though in doing so she brings out into the open their attendant problems, exposing the contradictions which the 'healthy' mind, that fiction of post-Freudian therapy, tries to repress (Goode, 1979: 104).

When Jude calls her a 'flirt', for example, Sue explodes like an Egerton heroine, explaining that she is much more complicated than this, full of shocking impulses unsuited to the 'social moulds civilization fits us into': 'I am not really Mrs Richard Phillotson, but a woman tossed about, all alone, with aberrant passions, and unaccountable antipathies' (*Jude*: 225–6). She is by no means uninterested in sex, shocking Jude by the list of erotic books she has read, starting with Lemprière and ending with the Bible, for she celebrates the Song of Solomon as a 'great and passionate song about ecstatic, natural human love' (172). She denies that she has any fear of men, insisting that women can decide whether or not the basis of a relationship is to be sexual:

> for no average man – no man short of a sensual savage – will molest a woman . . . unless she invites him. Until she says by a look 'Come on' he is always afraid to, and if you never say it, or look it, he never comes. (167–8)

She then tells the tale of her living in radical chastity with her undergraduate friend, vigorously insisting that her decision to preserve her virginity was not, as Jude claims, 'innocent':

> People say I must be cold-natured – sexless – on account of it. But I won't have it! Some of the most passionately erotic poets have been the most self-contained in their daily lives. (169)

Her own sexuality has clearly been of this cerebral sort.

Sue's liberated theories, of course, conflict with the repression of a society whose influence upon her own development she cannot avoid. When Jude meets her in Melchester, for example,

> Her hair, which formerly she had worn according to the custom of the day, was now twisted up tightly, and she had altogether the air of a woman clipped and pruned by severe discipline, an under-brightness shining through from the depths which that discipline had not yet been able to reach. (151)

This split in her personality is also reflected in the way she signs her letters, which alternate between warm acceptance of Jude's love – '*If you want to love me, Jude, you may* . . . Ever, Sue' (176) – and the more distant announcement of her accelerated marriage, signed in full: 'Susanna Florence Mary Bridehead'. Jude himself complains: 'I don't see why you sign your letter in such a new and terribly formal way? Surely you care a bit about me still' (190). And so she does, attempting to give it expression even after the wedding ceremony: 'her lips suddenly parted as if she were going to avow something. But she went on; and whatever she had meant to say remained unspoken' (195). She is not sufficiently liberated, on this occasion at least, to give voice to her attempted rebellion against Victorian values.

Sue's 'unconventionality', as she herself later admits, is 'theoretic' (243), based on the similarly mystical eroticism of her favourite poets, Swinburne and Shelley. In her, as in Shelley, desire demands more than physical consummation. She worships 'Venus Urania', the goddess of heavenly love, in which physical 'desire plays . . . only a secondary part', strongly objecting to the philosophy which 'only recognises relations based on animal desire' (188). In lines which echo Shelley's 'Epipsychidion' (LL: 78–9) she is called 'so ethereal a creature that her spirit could be seen trembling through her limbs' (*Jude*: 207). She urges Jude to quote the poem, even prompting him herself:

'There was a Being whom my spirit oft
Met on its visioned wanderings far aloft.

A seraph of Heaven, too gentle to be human,
Veiling beneath that radiant form of woman . . .'

O it is too flattering, so I won't go on! But say
it's me! – say it's me! (265)

Even Phillotson recognises that she and Jude are 'Shelleyan' in their love, like 'one person split in two'; 'they remind me of . . . Laon and Cythna' in *The Revolt of Islam* (250–2). Like Shelley's heroines Sue aims at immortality, a spiritual union emerging through but beyond the sexual out of the wreckage of social conventions.

Sue's romantic aspirations, however, founder upon the reality of natural and social laws, in particular those of sex and marriage. As Jude exclaims when he receives her letter announcing the imminence of her marriage to Phillotson, she does not know 'what marriage means' (189). She herself places the blame entirely on the institution. Of the many attacks she makes upon marriage, objecting to being given away 'like a she-ass or she-goat' (190), to being 'labelled "Phillotson"' (208), to being expected to give her love 'continuously to the chamber-officer appointed by the bishop's licence to receive it' (225), to being bound by 'a sordid contract' based on economic convenience and the social need that 'the male parent be known' (230) and by a 'vulgar . . . institution' which acts as 'a sort of trap to catch a man' (290), perhaps the most radical is her counter-suggestion based on the game played between power and desire analysed by Foucault:

If the marriage ceremony consisted in an oath and signed contract between the parties to cease loving from that day forward . . . and to avoid each other's society as much as possible in public, there would be more loving couples than there are now. Fancy the secret meetings between the perjuring husband and wife, the denials of having seen each other, the clambering in at bedroom windows, and the hiding in closets! There'd be little cooling then. (278)

It is a deliberately grotesque fantasy designed merely to mock the institution as it exists.

On the question of marriage Jude, the narrator and Hardy himself all agree with Sue. They certainly disagree with Gillingham's way of dealing with the New Woman: 'I think that she ought to be smacked, and brought to her senses' (253); and with Arabella's: 'I should have kept her chained on – her spirit for kicking would have been broke soon enough' (338). Hardy's letters of this period are full of complaints about the awfulness of marriage, that 'survival from the custom of capture and purchase, propped up by a theological superstition' (*CL* II: 296). He denied being 'an advocate of "free love"' since he was unable to envisage 'any possible scheme for the union of the sexes' (II: 122), although he was later to recommend 'collective social responsibility for children as a replacement for the family unity' (Boumelha, 1982: 151). The narrator in *Jude* expresses amazement at the way Jude and Arabella swear confidently in their marriage vows that 'they would assuredly believe, feel, and desire precisely as they had believed, felt, and desired during the few preceding weeks' (*Jude*: 78), poking fun too at the 'note of genuine wedlock', their violent quarrelling, which convinces a doubting landlord that they are indeed husband and wife (404). Jude himself, who sees his life as having been ruined by the attempt to base 'a permanent contract on a temporary feeling' (90), rebels against the turning of 'normal sex-impulses . . . into devilish domestic gins' (238).

All these objections to marriage make Jude and Sue resist the temptation to place their relationship on this institutional basis. There can be no doubting their desire for each other, although Hardy's constant revisions complicate matters. The first edition of the novel makes Sue colder and more reserved than in the serial, 'Hearts Insurgent' (Boumelha, 1982: 142), while the Wessex Edition reinstates some of her lost warmth and spontaneity, making her kiss 'close and long', for example, on parting from Jude to return to Phillotson after their aunt's funeral (*Jude*: 237; see Slack, 1956: 270–1). She is repelled by sex with Phillotson, driven to hysterical behaviour such as sleeping in the cupboard and leaping from the window to escape his embrace. As Hardy later insisted to Edmund Gosse, however, her sexual instinct is 'healthy so far as it goes', even if it is 'unusually weak and fastidious'. He went on to explain what he had been unable to make explicit in the novel, that her restriction of Jude's 'intimacies' to the occasional, 'even while they were living together', was designed to maintain her erotic power over him: 'while uncontracted she feels at liberty to yield herself as seldom as she chooses', thus keeping 'his passion as hot at the end as at the beginning' (*CL* II: 99).

Jude, understandably exasperated by this tantalising conduct, calls Sue 'incapable of real love' (*Jude*: 261), 'a disembodied creature' (265), 'bodiless' and lacking in 'animal passion' (279). Living 'with only a landing between them', the question of marriage (and with it, sex) is 'constantly on their minds'. She insists, however, on 'deciding how I'll live with you' (280), finally conceding only out of jealousy when Arabella returns. Again Hardy's revisions in the Wessex Edition make her more sympathetic: not only does she agree to sleep with Jude to prove that she is 'not a cold-hearted, sexless creature' but she gives unambiguous expression to her feelings, which makes 'a world of difference to Jude' (Slack, 1956: 272).

Hardy's depiction of Sue's sexual relations with Jude is necessarily indirect. When she finally capitulates, for example, Jude 'kissed her on one side, and on the other, and in the middle, and rebolted the front door' (*Jude*: 286). The rest is left to the reader's imagination. They continue to fight shy of marriage lest it kill their Shelleyan dream. Before their planned ceremony Sue demands to be kissed 'as a lover, incorporeally' (302) and, after deciding not to go through with it, they watch the contracting of another ill-matched pair with undisguised horror, kissing furtively behind a pillar before going home. Arabella, who sees them at the Great Wessex Agricultural Show, insists that Sue is ignorant of 'what I call love' (313) but the way in which she smiles after Jude pushes her nose into the roses reveals 'so much' about their new-found physical happiness (316).

These glimpses of sexual fulfilment on Sue's part are outweighed

in the reader's mind by the strength of her revulsion against it
following the traumatic death of her children – themselves, of
course, the product of her abandonment of radical chastity and
subsequent embroilment in the grind of childbirth and child-
rearing. Her later abrogation of all sexuality, 'the terrible flesh –
the curse of Adam' (364), like her symbolic tearing of the pretty
nightgown she had worn with Jude and adoption instead of an
'absolutely plain garment, of coarse and unbleached calico' (384),
represents a hysterical reaction to this tragedy, not her 'real' self.
For, as Jude himself insists, her 'natural instincts' were 'perfectly
healthy', if 'not quite as impassioned' as he might have wanted
(364). That her body is not brought into 'complete subjection' by
her fasting and prayer is clear from the way she implores Jude to
kiss her until he 'bruised her lips with kisses' on his final visit to
Marygreen (409). Her horrifying transformation of sexual relations
with her husband into a form of penance, shuddering and
clenching her teeth as she does her 'duty' (415–17), underlines the
failure of her attempted rebellion. 'Who were we', asks Jude, 'to
think we could act as pioneers' (372), although later he is less
self-critical, blaming society as much as their own lack of strength:
'the time was not ripe for us! Our ideas were fifty years too soon'
(419).

Sue's tragedy, then, is partly the result of social constraints,
particularly those of marriage. It is partly too, as in so many of
Hardy's novels, the fault of fate, in the form of Father Time. In
Sue's words,

> I said it was Nature's intention, Nature's law and *raison d'être*
> that we should be joyful in what instincts she afforded us –
> instincts which civilization had taken upon itself to thwart. . . .
> And now Fate has given us this stab in the back for being such
> fools as to take Nature at her word! (358)

Nature, as Jude so often realises, is not a reliable guide, showing
cruelty towards animals, 'scorn . . . for man's finer emotions, and a
lack of interest in his aspirations'. His particular wish, at this
point, is that Sue could bring forth children on her own, without
need of a father (197). Even the sexual relation itself, then,
deprived of the ideals of Shelley or the eroticism of Swinburne,
seen simply as part of the 'daily grind' of life, with 'its sure
stripping-away of all the romantic roles and fantasies with which

it is surrounded, becomes as grimy an aspect of the unfitness of things as any other' (Bayley, 1978: 206).

Jude and Father Time, by killing themselves, and Sue, by attempting to starve her sexual instincts, seem to take Schopenhauer's view that sex is the root of all evil (including the evil of life), leaving suffering humanity to be perpetuated by the disgusting Arabella, on the lookout for her next mate even as her last one lies dying. Arabella, of course, has the last word in this multivoiced text, insisting that Sue cannot find peace without sexual fulfilment. The New Woman, in other words, has failed to find a satisfactory answer to the old problem, not least because, in Hardy's bleak view, there is none.

# 9
# *The Well-Beloved*: The End of Art and Desire

Hardy's final novel, *The Well-Beloved*, is often ignored, seldom regarded as an important part of the canon. It is a fantastic tale, abandoning the constraints of realism against which Hardy's later work was forever struggling, a self-conscious farewell to fiction. Yet it has been seen as the key to his work, 'an interrogation of the relation between erotic fascination and creativity' which 'functions as an interpretation of the earlier novels or even as their parody', a final disclosure of the 'motivating energy of Hardy's fiction' (Miller, 1982: 148–51). Hardy told Florence Henniker that it was suggested by a sculptor's account of how he 'had often pursued a beautiful ear, nose, chin, &c, about London in omnibuses and on foot' (*CL* II: 169). But the many detailed similarities between descriptions of women in the novel and his notes for his own *Life* (Millgate, 1971: 300–2) leave little room for doubt that Jocelyn Pierston, the sculptor in the novel, the 'fantast' as he is called in the 'Preface', is based upon Hardy himself, even if the 'delicate dream' to which he gives 'objective continuity and a name' is 'more or less common to all men' (*WB*: 25).

The 'theory exhibited in *The Well-Beloved*', Hardy was later to write – having found it developed even further by Proust, himself a great admirer of this novel – is that love is an entirely subjective matter which creates the 'ideal beloved one' from its own resources, weaving erotic fantasies around its randomly chosen and unremarkable object (*Life*: 303, 466–7). Hardy's poem of the same title dramatises the split between the real external object and the imaginative construct. The persona, travelling towards his 'dear one', encounters a vision of 'perfect womankind' who insists that she is the true object of his love:

> Thou lovest what thou dreamest her:
> I am thy very dream!

The vision then vanishes and the bemused lover continues his journey, only to find his real bride

> pinched and thin,
> As if her soul had shrunk and died,
> And left a waste within. (*CP*: 121–3)

The real, in other words, cannot match the ideal, the image created by desire.

The plot of the novel, of which there are two versions, is somewhat more complex. The original serial, 'The Pursuit of the Well-Beloved', which appeared in the *Illustrated London News* in 1892, stresses the absurdity of marriage. The hero, engaged to the young Avice Caro, runs away and marries the more glamorous Marcia Bencomb, but their passion turns to bitterness in a matter of days and they agree to separate. 'Was there anything more absurd,' asks Marcia, than that 'grey-headed legislators from time immemorial should have gravely based inflexible laws upon the ridiculous dream of young people that a transient mutual desire for each other was going to last forever?' (*WB*: 223). Believing Marcia to be dead, Pearston, as he is spelt in the serial, falls in love at twenty-year intervals and in between other infatuations not only with Avice's daughter but with her daughter too, the original Avice's granddaughter, whom he eventually marries, only to release her from the bond on discovering that she has a much more suitable lover, a young man who turns out to be Marcia's son. Pearston attempts suicide, sailing out alone into the fatal waters of The Race from which he is rescued and then nursed back to health by his first wife, still alive but transformed into 'a wrinkled crone, with a pointed chin, her figure bowed, her hair white as snow'. The final line of the serial records Pearston's hysterical laughter at 'the grotesqueness of things', in particular the changes that have overtaken the object of his desire (248–9).

The revised version of the novel, published in book form in 1897, plays down the theme of marriage, the only marriage that takes place being at the end when Pierston settles down comfortably with Marcia, having lost all sexual desire and with it all artistic susceptibility. The connection between the two, implicit in the serial version, is made more explicit in the novel, which becomes in the process not only another study of desire in all its absurd and uncontrollable manifestations but a recognition of the erotic source of artistic creativity.

'The Well-Beloved' is the name Pierston gives to the 'elusive idealization he called his Love, who, ever since his boyhood, had flitted from human shell to human shell an indefinite number of times' (31). The serial version makes the point dramatically by presenting the young sculptor in the act of burning, or attempting to burn, 'several packets of love-letters, in sundry hands'. The different styles of writing, however, recall the tender sentiments which once went with them, and he resolves to proceed no further:

> That packet, at least, he would preserve for the writer's sake, notwithstanding that the person of the writer, wherever she might be, was now but as an empty shell which had once contained his ideal for a transient time. (217)

Another packet contains some hair, part of the actual body whose 'curves' he had 'worked into statuettes', so he abandons the task altogether. It is against this background that he meets the first Avice, whose innocent kiss to her returned childhood companion sparks off his introspective questioning whether or not the Well-Beloved is taking abode in her body. He returns her kiss, less innocently, still surrounded by unburnt letters which make her realise: 'I am – only one – in a long long row!' while 'the ghosts of Isabella, Florence, Winifred, Lucy, Jane, and Evangeline . . . seemed to rise . . . from the flames' (219).

In both serial and novel Pierston finds himself proposing to his childhood friend, 'full of misgiving' about the possible consequences. It is not that any of his former flames would intervene:

> For he had quite disabused his mind of the assumption that the idol of his fancy was an integral part of the personality in which it had sojourned for a long or a short while. . . . Each individuality . . . had been merely a transient condition of her. . . . Essentially she was perhaps of no tangible substance; a spirit, a dream, a frenzy, a conception, an aroma, an epitomized sex, a light of the eye, a parting of the lips. God only knew what she really was; Pierston did not. She was indescribable. (34)

The stable conditions of normal personal relations are totally distorted by the descent of this divinity he dreams of as Aphrodite, symbolising the power, the uncontrollability and the fragility of desire. Avice Caro, who 'was, in truth, what is called a "nice" girl . . . one of the class with whom the risks of matrimony appropriate most nearly to zero' (35), seems to have little connection with these troublesome depths.

It is scarcely surprising, then, that the Well-Beloved hovers only briefly over Avice Caro before descending more firmly upon Marcia Bencomb, an altogether more promising object of Pierston's erotic interest, encountered in suitably stormy conditions as he returns from Portland across the Pebble Bank to the mainland. Her profile immediately strikes him as 'dignified, arresting, that of a very Juno' (41) and when they are forced to take shelter together in the limited space afforded by an overturned hull her attractions prove irresistible. They crouch 'so close to each other that he could feel her furs against him' and catch 'the suppressed gasp of passionateness in her utterance' (44). When they continue their journey she makes no objection to his arm 'encircling her waist' (46). Alert to 'a possible migration of the Well-Beloved',

> he went on thinking how soft and warm the lady was in her fur covering, as he held her so tightly; the only dry spots in the clothing of either being her left side and his right, where they excluded the rain by their mutual pressure. (47)

His fetishistic imagination is given full rein when, on arriving at an inn, he takes over from the maid the responsibility of drying Marcia's damp clothes before the fire, 'overhauling the robes and extending them one by one'. As the steam rises from her garments he falls into an 'reverie' from which he emerges after ten minutes in full adoration of his newly beloved (48).

The suddenness of Pierston's turning from the nice but familiar Avice to the more mysterious Marcia provokes a confession to his fellow-painter Somers in the course of which he enumerates the many previous 'incarnations' of his divinity. The first, when he was nine, took the form of 'a little blue-eyed girl of eight'; the second, some months later, a girl who smiled at him from a horse; and so on, following very much the pattern of Hardy's own life. Visitations four to thirteen took place in his early teens:

> Four times she masqueraded as a brunette, twice as a pale-haired creature, and two or three times under a complexion neither light nor dark. Sometimes she was a tall, fine girl, but

more often, I think, she preferred to slip into the skin of a lithe
airy being, of no great stature. (57)

Each time, however, she vanished as quickly as she came, leaving
the remaining body a mere 'relic' or 'corpse' (58). Pierston feels
these uncontrollable desires to be so monstrous that he had been
afraid to confess even to his friend 'the manner of man I am . . . I
lie awake thinking about it' (52). Somers, however, assures him
that he is quite normal: 'You are like other men, only rather worse.
Essentially, all men are fickle, like you; but not with such percep-
tiveness' (58). The suggestion here, as in Freud, is that the
characteristics seen at their extreme in artistic temperaments such
as Pierston or Hardy can be found to some extent in everyone.

The Well-Beloved remains attached to Marcia for a year or so
after the couple agree to separate, although even during this
period 'the Phantom' threatens the occasional distant appearance,
'at the end of a street, on the far sands of a shore, in a window, in a
meadow, at the opposite side of a railway station' (66). For a time
he resists her lure but the 'ever-bubbling spring of emotion'
which he pours into his art feeds on the images of women seen:

> The study of beauty was his only joy for years onward. In the
> streets he would observe a face, or a fraction of a face, which
> seemed to express to a hair's breadth in mutable flesh what he
> was at that moment wishing to express in durable shape. He
> would dodge and follow the owner like a detective; in omnibus,
> in cab, in steam-boat, through crowds, into shops, churches,
> theatres, public-houses, and slums – mostly, when at close
> quarters, to be disappointed for his pains. (67)

Distance and inaccessibility, then, are vital; contact is disastrous.

'The Well-Beloved' flits from actresses to fashionable ladies to
shop-girls. 'Once she was a dancing-girl at the Royal Moorish
Palace of Varieties' whom he steadfastly avoided meeting, for he
realised that to talk with 'the substance would send the elusive
haunter scurrying fearfully away into some other even less accessible mask-figure' (68). The women he sees are always masks,
screens, images and signs to be filled with personal meaning and
transformed into art: 'For all these dreams he translated into
plaster', becoming highly successful by 'hitting a public taste' fed
by similar desires (68), 'modelling and chipping his ephemeral
fancies into perennial shapes' (72).

The ultimate in inaccessibility is death, which brings to the first Avice an attraction she never had before. As Pierston studies a photograph of her he realises that 'he loved the woman dead and inaccessible as he had never loved her in life', rejoicing in the 'purity of this new-sprung affection' from which the 'flesh was absent altogether' (88). Although this immediately banishes all thoughts of the 'soft and sylph-like' Nicola Pine-Avon (75), another temporary resting place for the Well-Beloved, it does not prevent him from courting the second Avice Caro, who is prettier but stupider than her mother. To begin with Pierston keeps his distance, peeping through the windows of her cottage and gazing with longing as the lamplit laundress does her ironing, her face 'warm and pink with her exertions and the heat of the stove' (100). But he proceeds to manufacture meetings, ostensibly to discuss her linen or to help her fasten her sheets, in the course of which the accidental contact of their fingers causes him much erotic excitement. He agonises over the folly of pursuing a young girl separated from him not only by age but by class and intellect. He also recognises that she is 'colder in nature' and 'commoner in character' than her mother:

> He was wretched for hours. Yet he would not have stood where he did stand in the ranks of an imaginative profession if he had not been at the mercy of every haunting of the fancy that can beset man. It was in his weaknesses as a citizen and a national-unit that his strength lay as an artist. (110)

It is difficult not to see in this passage a certain self-justification on the part not only of the narrator but of the author.

The irony is that the second Avice suffers exactly the same syndrome of perpetually displaced desire. She confesses to tiring of her lovers as soon as she gets to know them but Pierston, who finds himself already one of the 'corpses' of her 'ideal inhabitant' (114), continues to pursue her. He follows her as she pants up a hill to visit a soldier,

> for the moment an irradiated being, the epitome of a whole sex: by the beams of his own infatuation
> > 'robed in such exceeding glory
> > That he beheld her not';
> beheld her not as she really was. (117)

He gazes at her 'still gazing at the soldier', the absurdity of their classic triangle of desire failing to prevent his Shelleyan idealisation of the commonplace object of his attentions.

Proximity without possession tantalises Pierston still further when he persuades the naive local girl to keep house for him in London, where he has ample opportunity to study her beauty,

> the charm of her bending profile; the well-characterized though softly lined nose, the round chin with, as it were, a second leap in the curve to the throat, and the sweep of the eyelashes over the rosy cheek during the sedulously lowered glance. How futilely he had laboured to express the character of that face in clay, and, while catching it in substance, had yet lost something that was essential! (130)

It is that elusive quality which art and desire seek, that sense of imperfection and incompleteness which they share.

It is not only the sight but even the slightest sounds that Avice makes which trigger off the sculptor's erotic susceptibility, 'the pit-pat of naked feet, accompanied by the brushing of drapery' as she goes in the middle of the night to release a mouse caught in its trap and the 'soft breathing' that emerges from her room 'like that of an infant' (134–5). This erotic idyll ends, however, when Pierston discovers that she is already married (not to the soldier, of course, but to a disgruntled quarryman to whom the disappointed artist returns her). His only condition is that she christen her daughter Avice, after which he departs with the words 'Here endeth the dream' (144).

This third Avice, however, is destined to provide yet another erotic dream on Pierston's return to his native island after another twenty-year absence. She is a 'ladylike creature . . . altogether finer in figure than her mother or grandmother' but in other respects 'the very she . . . who had kissed him forty years before' (153). The similarity of features, he recognises, 'helped the dream', which he cannot but feel as foolish. But he remains 'subject to gigantic fantasies', bowing to the moon as a symbol of his inconstant desire and of his double-edged artistic susceptibility, which is both a 'curse' and a 'blessing' (156). On rescuing his 'belated edition of the beloved' from the rocks by removing her feet from her 'pretty boot' (which he then pockets for future fetishistic meditation) he continues to ask why he was born with such a temperament, which continues in age as in youth to compel him to pursue his 'desire in the face of his understanding' (173). In the Lacanian symbol so often used in the earlier novels, Pierston's reflection in the mirror surprises him into a sense of the split in his personality between what he appears from the outside and what he feels:

The person he appeared was too grievously far, chronologically, in advance of the person he felt himself to be . . . never had he seemed so aged by a score of years as he was represented in the glass in that cold grey morning light. While his soul was what it was, why should he have been encumbered with that withering carcase, without the ability to shift it off for another, as his ideal Beloved had so frequently done? (170)

In fact, after the third Avice elopes with her Jersey lover (Marcia's stepson) Pierston does become a different person. He awakens from a fever to find himself 'no longer the same man that he had hitherto been':

The artistic sense had left him, and he could no longer attach a definite sentiment to images of beauty recalled from the past. His appreciativeness was capable of examining itself only on utilitarian matters . . .
    At first he was appalled; and then he said 'Thank God!' (198–9)

He is capable of discerning the ravages of time upon Marcia's face, 'the raspings, chisellings, scourgings, bakings, freezings of forty invidious years', cruelly exposed by the morning sun, with a measure of equanimity (201) and the former lovers finally enter upon a marriage of convenience.

As a final confirmation of his changed personality Pierston, thoroughly disgusted by his own sculptures, tests his taste in painting by a visit to the National Gallery where, as expected, 'He saw no more to move him . . . in the time-defying presentations of Perugino, Titian, Sebastiano . . . than in the work of the pavement artist they had passed on their way' (202). Far from regretting this, however, he rejoices at the death of the susceptibility to beauty he sees as responsible for his 'greatest sorrows'. 'Thank Heaven I am old at last,' he exclaims. 'The curse is removed' (202). He settles into his boring marriage, to be 'sometimes mentioned' by young art critics as 'a man not without genius, whose powers were insufficiently recognized in his lifetime' (206). His other major achievement, significantly, is 'the closing of the old natural fountains' in the main street of his native island 'because of their possible contamination' and their replacement with less danger-ous pipes (205). With the death of desire comes the end of inspiration.

It is possible to read the ending of the novel (though not the serial) positively. The suggestion, as at the end of *Far from the Madding Crowd*, is that marriage can work only if it is based upon admiration rather than desire, friendship rather than love: 'I have no love to give you,' Pierston tells Marcia. 'But such friendship as I am capable of is yours to the end' (204). If this is positive, however, it is so only in the resigned manner of Schopenhauer, for whom the only hope for mankind lay in the extinction of the sexual instinct and of 'those exuberant feelings and supersensible soap-bubbles of romance' (Dave, 1985: 106). This certainly is the sense of the last line of the serial version, Pierston's hysterical recognition of the absurdity of 'this ending to my would-be romantic history' (WB: 249). For Schopenhauer, in *The Metaphysics of the Love of the Sexes*, love was an illusion by which the individual was made 'the dupe of the species'. The dream – always to be disappointed – that possession of the desired object would bring extraordinary happiness results only in bringing together for life lovers united only by sexual desire, which is the means by which mankind is cheated into perpetuating his misery, making the pattern of mortal agony immortal upon the earth (Dave, 1985: 100–7).

This is precisely what the narrator suggests when Pierston is pursuing the second Avice, the little laundress, fully aware as he is of her incompatibility as a companion: 'Nature was working her plans for the next generation under the cloak of a dialogue upon linen' (WB: 102). Marcia Bencomb too, soon disillusioned in love, expresses a decidedly bitter view of romance, envying the lot of those classic lovers similarly affected by family disputes, Romeo and Juliet:

It was a fortunate thing for the affections of these two Veronese lovers that they died when they did. In a short time the enmity of their families would have proved a fruitful source of dissension; Juliet would have gone back to her people, he to his; the subject would have split them as it splits us. (63)

All Hardy's lovers can be seen to have been split by desire, their seemingly stable identities shattered by instincts beyond their control. The only escape for them lies in death: literally as in Pierston's suicide attempt, or metaphorically with the death of desire and of creative energy.

Even the geographical setting of this novel, Portland Bill, can be seen as a symbolic representation of the sexual instinct responsible for reproduction and the continuation of life. It is a phallic promontory of 'oolite' or eggstone jutting into the maternal sea, whose moans of 'travail' mingle with those of the second Avice as she gives birth to her daughter (141). But the 'eggs' of the rock, the ossified bones of tiny sea-creatures, are 'not the beginning of a new life cycle but the dead remnants of one passed through' (Miller, 1982: 164), in the words of Shelley quoted on the opening page of the novel,

> The melancholy ruins
> Of cancelled cycles. (*WB*: 28)

The cycles of Pierston's returning desire take place, then, upon a peninsula itself composed of endless cycles of life persisting beyond the death of the individual.

'Pierston-Hardy', as John Fowles called the autobiographical persona of the novel, 'feels cursed by his "inability to ossify", to mature like other men.' Yet when he does so, he dies as an artist (Fowles, 1977b: 29). His death-wish, however, cannot altogether extinguish his positive qualities. In the serial version he fails to commit suicide and in the novel his work continues to be appreciated by others. Hardy's own farewell to fiction, similarly, cannot put an end to the chain of creativity which continues in his readers and critics. Having laid bare the motivation of his own fiction, he can himself refuse to write any more novels; but he cannot actually terminate the constant reformulation of the patterns of desire, the endless cycle of interpretation generated by his work (Miller, 1982: 173–4), of which this book is one example among many.

Even this book, however, cannot claim to explain desire or art, merely to illustrate their interconnection. *The Well-Beloved* has been called 'the closest conducted tour we shall ever have of the psychic processes behind Hardy's written product', his quest for that sense of perfection and completion experienced at the mother's breast and constantly sought in sexual and artistic fulfilment (Fowles, 1977b: 30–3). Some critics such as Hillis Miller and René Girard argue that this sense of lack, of absence, of imperfection, is fundamentally metaphysical and can achieve resolution only in religious belief. Failing to find God, the final guarantor of meaning, unity and completion, Hardy, they argue, was doomed to the perpetually disappointing cycles of desire for which the compulsive repetition of his fiction was only a displaced resolution. Whether this is true or not, what remains without question is the fundamentally erotic nature of Hardy's fiction, a monument to both art and desire.

# Bibliography

Place of publication is London unless otherwise specified. All references to Hardy's novels, with self-evident abbreviations, are to the paperback version of the New Wessex Edition (1974–5), apart from *An Indiscretion in the Life of an Heiress* (Hutchinson, 1976), *Life's Little Ironies* and *A Group of Noble Dames*, both in the Pocket Classics series (Gloucester, 1983) and *A Changed Man* (Wessex Edition, 1914).

Other works by Hardy include

1  *CL = The Collected Letters of Thomas Hardy*, ed. Richard Little Purdy and Michael Millgate, 7 vols (Oxford, 1978–88).
2  *CP = The Collected Poems of Thomas Hardy*, (1930).
3  Hardy (1894) 'The Tree of Knowledge', *New Review*, 10: 681.
4  *Life = The Life and Work of Thomas Hardy by Thomas Hardy*, ed. Michael Millgate (1984).
5  *PN* (1978) *The Personal Notebooks of Thomas Hardy*, ed. Richard Taylor.
6  *PW* (1967) *Thomas Hardy's Personal Writings*, ed. Harold Orel.

*THA* refers to the *Thomas Hardy Annual*, ed. Norman Page, 5 vols (1982–7).

## OTHER WORKS

Barthes, Roland (1975) *S/Z*, trans. Richard Miller.
Barthes, Roland (1976) *The Pleasure of the Text*, trans. Richard Miller.
Barthes, Roland (1979) *A Lover's Discourse*, trans. Richard Howard.
Bayley, John (1978) *An Essay on Hardy* (Cambridge).
Bayley, John (1982) 'The Love Story in *Two on a Tower*', *THA*, 1: 60–70.
Beckett, Samuel [1931] (1965) *Proust*.
Belsey, Catherine (1980) *Critical Practice*.
Black, Peter (1973) 'Wessexuality', *Listener*, 90: 796–7.
Blake, Kathleen (1982) 'Pure Tess: Hardy on Knowing a Woman', *Studies in English Literature*, 22: 689–705.
Blake, Kathleen (1983) *Love and the Woman Question in Victorian Literature* (Brighton).
Blunden, Edmund (1941) *Thomas Hardy*.
Boumelha, Penny (1982) *Thomas Hardy and Women* (Brighton).
Bradbury, Malcolm (1984) 'Terminal Sex', *Observer*, 1 April 1984.
Brady, Kristin (1982) *The Short Stories of Thomas Hardy* (New York).

Brady, Kristin (1986) 'Tess and Alec: Rape or Seduction?', *THA*, 4: 124–47.
Bullen, J.B. (1986) *The Expressive Eye: Fiction and Perception in the Work of Thomas Hardy* (Oxford).
Bullen, J.B. (1987) 'Review Essay: The Buried Life: A New Edition of F.E. Hardy's "Biography"', *THA*, 5:187–96.
Burgess, Anthony (1985) 'Locutions of Sex and Death', *The Times Literary Supplement*, 12 April 1985: 399.
Butler, Lance St John (ed.) (1977) *Thomas Hardy After Fifty Years*.
Casagrande, Peter J. (1982) *Unity in Hardy's Novels: 'Repetitive Symmetries'*.
Charney, Maurice (1981) *Sexual Fiction*.
Cox, R.G. (ed.) (1970) *Thomas Hardy: The Critical Heritage* (New York).
Cunningham, A.R. (1973) 'The "New Woman Fiction" of the 1890's', *Victorian Studies*, 17: 177–85.
Dave, Jagdish Chandra (1985) *The Human Predicament in Hardy's Novels*.
Davis, W. Eugene (1968) '*Tess of the d'Urbervilles*: Some Ambiguities about a Pure Woman', *Nineteenth Century Fiction*, 22: 397–401.
Edwards, Carol and Duane (1980) '*Jude the Obscure*: A Psychoanalytic Study', *Hartford Studies in Literature*, 13: 78–90.
Egerton, George (1894) *Keynotes*.
Eliot, T.S. (1934) *After Strange Gods*.
Foucault, Michel (1984, 1987, 1988) *The History of Sexuality*, trans. Robert Hurley, 3 vols (Harmondsworth).
Fowles, John [1969] (1977a) *The French Lieutenant's Woman*.
Fowles, John (1977b) 'Hardy and the Hag', in Butler (1977): 28–42.
Freud, Sigmund (1977) *On Sexuality*, trans. James Strachey, ed. Angela Richards, vol. 7 of the Pelican Freud Library.
Gay, Peter (1984, 1986) *The Bourgeois Experience: From Victoria to Freud*, 2 vols (Oxford).
Girard, René (1965) *Deceit, Desire and the Novel: Self and Other in Literary Structure*, trans. Yvonne Freccero (Baltimore).
Gittings, Robert (1978) *Young Thomas Hardy*.
Gittings, Robert (1980) *The Older Hardy*.
Goode, John (1979) 'Sue Bridehead and the New Woman', in Jacobus (1979).
Gregor, Ian (1974) *The Great Web: The Form of Hardy's Major Fiction*.
Grindle, Juliet and Gatrell, Simon (1983) 'General Introduction' to *Tess of the d'Urbervilles*, (Oxford).
Grundy, Joan (1979) *Hardy and the Sister Arts*.
Guerard, Albert J. (1949) *Thomas Hardy: The Novels and Stories*.
Guerard, Albert J. (ed.) (1963) *Hardy: A Collection of Critical Essays* (Englewood Cliffs, New Jersey).
Hassett, Michael (1971) 'Compromised Romanticism in *Jude the Obscure*', *Nineteenth Century Fiction*, 25: 432–43.
Heath, Stephen (1982) *The Sexual Fix*.
Heilman, Robert (1966) 'Hardy's Sue Bridehead', *Nineteenth Century Fiction*, 20: 307–23.
Howe, Irving (1968) *Thomas Hardy*.
Hyde, W.J. (1969) 'Thomas Hardy: The Poor Man and the Deterioration of

His Ladies', *Victorian Newsletter*, 36: 14–18.
Jackson, Arlene M. (1981) *Illustration and the Novels of Thomas Hardy* (Totowa, New Jersey).
Jacobson, Howard (1984) *Peeping Tom.*
Jacobson, Howard (1985) 'Himself on Himself', *The Times Literary Supplement*, 7 June 1985: 625.
Jacobus, Mary (1975) 'Sue the Obscure', *Essays in Criticism*, 25: 304–28.
Jacobus, Mary (1976) 'Tess's Purity' *Essays in Criticism*, 26: 318–38.
Jacobus, Mary (ed.) (1979) *Women Writing and Writing about Women.*
Jakobson, Roman and Halle, Morris (1956) *Fundamentals of Language* (The Hague).
Keys, Romey T. (1985) 'Hardy's Uncanny Narrative: A Reading of "The Withered Arm"', *Texas Studies in Literature and Language*, 27: 106–23.
Kramer, Dale (ed.) (1979) *Critical Approaches to the Fiction of Thomas Hardy.*
Kramer, Dale (ed.) (1981) Clarendon Edition of *The Woodlanders* (Oxford).
Kristeva, Julia (1980) *Desire in Language: A Semiotic Approach to Literature and Art* (New York).
Lacan, Jacques (1968) *The Language of the Self*, trans. with notes and commentary by Anthony Wilden.
Lacan, Jacques (1979) *The Four Fundamental Concepts of Psychoanalysis*, trans. Alan Sheridan.
Laird, J.T. (1975) *The Shaping of 'Tess of the d'Urbervilles'* (Oxford).
Langland, Elizabeth (1980) 'A Perspective of One's Own: Thomas Hardy and the Elusive Sue Bridehead', *Studies in the Novel*, 12: 12–28.
Larkin, Philip (1983) *Required Writing.*
Lawrence, D.H. (1978) *Phoenix*, ed. Edward D. McDonald.
Leavis, L.R. (1985) 'The Late Nineteenth-Century Novel and the Change Towards the Sexual – Gissing, Hardy, Lawrence', *English Studies*, 66: 36–47.
Lemon, Lee and Reis, Marion (eds) (1965) *Russian Formalist Criticism: Four Essays* (Lincoln, Nebraska).
Lodge, David (1981) *Working with Structuralism.*
Lodge, David (1984) *Small World.*
Loth, David (1962) *The Erotic in Literature.*
Lucas, John (1977) *The Literature of Change* (Brighton and New York).
McGhee, Richard D. (1984) '"Swinburne Planteth, Hardy Watereth": Victorian Views of Pain and Pleasure in Human Sexuality', *Tennessee Studies in Literature*, 27: 83–107.
Macherey, Pierre (1978) *A Theory of Literary Production*, trans. Geoffrey Wall.
Marcus, Stephen [1966] (1969) *The Other Victorians: A Study of Sexuality and Pornography in Mid-Nineteenth-Century England.*
Marcus, Stephen (1984) *Freud and the Culture of Psychoanalysis: Studies in the Transition from Victorian Humanism to Modernity* (Boston).
May, Charles E. (1974) 'Hardy's Diabolical Dames: A Generic Consideration', *Genre*, 7: 307–21.
Meisel, Perry (1972) *Thomas Hardy: The Return of the Repressed* (New Haven).

Milberg-Kaye, Ruth (1983) *Thomas Hardy: Myths of Sexuality* (New York).

Miller, J. Hillis (1970) *Thomas Hardy: Distance and Desire* (Cambridge, Massachusetts).

Miller, J. Hillis (1982) *Fiction and Repetition: Seven English Novels* (Oxford).

Millett, Kate (1977) *Sexual Politics*.

Millgate, Michael (1971) *Thomas Hardy: His Career as a Novelist*.

Millgate, Michael (1982) *Thomas Hardy: A Biography* (Oxford).

Morgan, Charles (1943) *The House of Macmillan*.

Morgan, Rosemarie (1987) 'Inscriptions of Self: Thomas Hardy and Autobiography', *THA*, 5: 137–56.

Noble, James Ashcroft (1895) 'The Fiction of Sexuality', *Contemporary Review*, 67: 490–8.

Oliphant, Margaret (1896) 'The Anti-Marriage League', *Blackwood's Magazine*, 159: 135–49.

Page, Norman (1977) *Thomas Hardy*.

Paterson, John (1960) *The Making of 'The Return of the Native'* (Berkeley and Los Angeles).

Poole, Adrian (1981)'"Men's Words" and Hardy's Women', *Essays in Criticism*, 31: 328–45.

Rabiger, Michael (1985) 'Tess and Saint Tryphena: Two Pure Women Faithfully Presented', *THA*, 3: 54–73.

Rogers, Katharine (1975) 'Women in Thomas Hardy', *Contemporary Review*, 19: 249–58.

Sheridan, Alan (1980) *Michel Foucault: The Will to Truth*.

Shklovsky, Victor (1965) 'Art as Technique', in Lemon and Reis (1965): 3–24.

Showalter, Elaine (1979) 'The Unmanning of the Mayor of Casterbridge', in Kramer (1979): 101–112.

Silverman, Kaja (1984) 'History, Figuration and Female Subjectivity in *Tess of the d'Urbervilles'*, *Novel*, 18: 5–28.

Slack, Robert (1956) 'The Text of Hardy's *Jude the Obscure'*, *Nineteenth Century Fiction*, 11: 261–75.

Smith, Anne (ed.) (1979) *The Novels of Thomas Hardy*.

Sontag, Susan (1967) 'The Pornographic Imagination', *Partisan Review*, 34: 161–212.

Stewart, J.I.M. (1971) *Thomas Hardy: A Critical Biography*.

Stubbs, Patricia (1979) *Women and Fiction: Feminism and the Novel 1880–1920*.

Stutfield, Hugh (1895) 'Tommyrotics', *Blackwood's Magazine*, 157: 833–45.

Sumner, Rosemary (1980) 'Hardy Ahead of His Time: "Barbara of the House of Grebe"', *Notes and Queries* 225: 230–1.

Sumner, Rosemary (1981) *Thomas Hardy: Psychological Novelist*.

Sumner, Rosemary (1982) 'The Experimental and the Absurd in *Two on a Tower'*, *THA*, 1: 71–81.

Tanner, Tony (1968) 'Colour and Movement in Hardy's *Tess of the d'Urbervilles'*, *Critical Quarterly*, 10: 219–39.

Taylor, Richard H. (1982) *The Neglected Hardy: Thomas Hardy's Lesser Novels*.

Thurley, Geoffrey (1975) *The Psychology of Hardy's Novels* (St Lucia, Queensland).

Waldoff, Leon (1979) 'Psychological Determinism in *Tess of the d'Urbervilles*', in Kramer (1979): 135–54.

Watt, George (1984) *The Fallen Woman in the Nineteenth-Century English Novel* (Beckenham).

Weinstein, Philip (1984) *The Semantics of Desire: Changing Models of Identity from Dickens to Joyce* (Princeton, New Jersey).

Williams, Merryn (1982) 'Hardy and the Woman Question', *THA*, 1: 44–59.

Williams, Merryn (1984) *Women in the English Novel, 1800–1900* (New York).

Wittenberg, Judith Bryant (1982) 'Early Hardy Novels and the Fictional Eye', *Novel*, 16: 157–64.

Wright, Elizabeth (1984) *Psychoanalytic Criticism*.

Young, Robert (ed.) (1981) *Untying the Text*.

# Index